# live your best life.

## by michele jones

First published in 2015 by

For You Corporation Pty Ltd.
PO Box 31
Toronto, NSW, Australia 2283

Australia * New Zealand * Indonesia * Malaysia * Singapore * Philippines
* United Kingdom * USA

© For You Corporation Pty Ltd.
The moral rights of the author have been asserted.

National Library of Australia Cataloguing-in-Publication data:

| | |
|---|---|
| *Author:* | Jones, Michele |
| *Title:* | Live Your Best Life / Michele Jones |
| *ISBN 13:* | 978-1514315118 |
| *ISBN-10:* | 1514315114 |
| *Subjects:* | Mind, Body, Spirit |
| | Self Help |
| | Motivation (Psychology) |
| | Life Skills |
| | Coaching |
| | Personal Coaching |
| | Attitude (Psychology) |

*Editor-in-chief:* Maria Martello
**Cover Design:** Bliss Inventive

**This book is part of the SpiritCast Network of Books, visit
www.spiritcastnetwork.com.au**

# Dedication

This book is dedicated to my life so far on this planet and to all the wonderful people I have met and am still yet to meet along the way, who everyday provide me with the lessons I know I was sent here to learn and to pass onto others.

This book is also an acknowledgement of gratitude to all the coaches out there in the world who are dedicated to assisting others to achieve and live their dreams – complete love and respect for all you do.

And finally, to you, the reader, the client, the friend, the stranger in the street, the person I am still yet to meet in person, this book has been written with love **FOR YOU,** for I believe we are all family.

*May you all "Live Your Best Life" always.*

# Table of Contents

# WELCOME

# WHAT DOES IT MEAN TO LIVE YOUR BEST LIFE?

And, how will you know when you are living your best life?

More importantly, what will it take for you to live your best life?

The concept of living your best life implies that there is in fact a plan for you to do so. I believe there is one and it is up to you whether you want to participate in it or not. It's entirely up to you, as if you are purchasing your very own 'general admission' ticket to the movie of your life, you know, the one with the happy ending?

The blueprint of your plan is not a rigid, predestined, one-option-only plan, but rather a structure from which to create the future of your choice. After all, isn't this why you were born? It's a structure that holds the clues to comfort and happiness in your own skin and the pathway for you to live your best life.

Without guidance, though, we're often unable to see this best life easily in front of us. So we cling to the conventional models of achieving success, such as what we see our friends, family and colleagues doing and the messages that the media send. We work hard, we schmooze the boss, we try to be model parents, we try to be good. Striving in these ways makes us feel that we're working toward something productive, but it also ultimately makes us feel that we are chasing our tails, doing more to be 'successful' so that we can earn our time to relax and enjoy - a time that for most of us never seems to come.

A much easier way to 'have it all' is within our reach.

When we learn to see our life's mission and plan, we can structure our lives according to that deep-seated plan, so that we can find the most organic and true version of our personal and professional success. This means not just being happy and successful, but living a life in which these good things come to you easily, without the stress, strain, strife, or effort that you may have come to accept as a 'normal' part of your life and reality.

Being happy doesn't have to be hard or fake...there is a way to truly be happy.

And I get this, because for years I have had many people disbelieve that I could actually be as happy as I am.

I believe we all possess an internally wired compass that we were born with; our own GPS that points us to our own individual wisdom that is programmed to point us to the things that most fulfil us.

I also believe that personal and professional satisfaction comes from tapping into this (and yes, Dave Thompson, I did just think of you tapping open a coconut!)

Reaching a state of ease is what the journey you will take with me as your 'Live Your Best Life Coach' is all about. If you like, you can even call me your LYBL Coach, if you want it to sound even cooler, like some secret group or club of which you are part.

Together, on your journey through this book you will work to discover a point where your life just seems to 'click'. No-one will have to tell you when that happens — you'll know your life is clicking because you'll have nothing to complain about. Boring right? I mean, how will you even know what to talk about if there is nothing to complain about? The stillness that you will find in your mind will become your gateway to inner peace and your ultimate happiness.

So, how do you learn to even begin to identify your best life, when up until now this has merely been a dream? How do you reach this most organic and true version of yourself which aligns with your meaning of success?

Well, I believe it involves becoming able to listen to your very own wisdom, the wisdom with which you were born, and that as you have grown through all of your life's experiences, has been lost within you. You simply have to find a way to reconnect with it. A wisdom for which you are innately wired, a wisdom that holds the answers to your quest for satisfaction in your life. Learning to access, activate and apply that wisdom is how you will reach the ease and satisfaction I am promising to you is there.

*Live Your Best Life* is not intended to be a prescription for overcoming sexual abuse, cancer or obesity. Throughout this book I will share my personal battles and struggles throughout the pages, only in the hope that my own experiences can serve as a metaphor for whatever personal and professional obstacles you may be facing in your own life. There may even be that one story you needed to hear in order to relate to, to make it real. By using my skills as a life, business, executive and professional coach on our journey together, I will take you through a process that will assist you to overcome any obstacles that lie between you and your best life; and I will do this in a way as if you are sitting right beside me, as if we have known each other for years, and you will feel that I simply just get you. Because, I do.

This journey is one you will take within, instead of looking outward to the model or rules of others for the solutions (I know, sounds weird when the models and systems are what I have coached on for almost three decades). I have come to understand and believe that by you using what is already within you – the very resources you were born with — your very own innate wisdom — that you will save time, energy and money. You'll stop doing umpteen, million, billion, trillion things in pursuit of what you believe you want, and instead you will unleash your own secret powers — your own innate wisdom. As you do this, you will fire up your own personal power and allow your built-in extraordinary life, that one that has been lying dormant, simply waiting for you to arrive, to evolve as it was designed and meant to.

Whether you are a corporate executive, a budding entrepreneur, a Gen Y'er, a housewife or a dog trainer, as your LYBL Coach I will assist you to get in touch with who you really are and what you really want. I will help reflect your inner wisdom outwards, where you can finally hear it with great clarity and certainty and in a way that you will finally understand. It will speak directly to you.

Through this book, I'll offer you support, permission to shine again (because so many of us need it) and a clear structure through which to follow that wisdom to successes that might ordinarily have been held within your wildest dreams.

Actually…let's even go beyond those!

You'll get to meet a number of clients along the way that will share their stories and journeys with you that will serve to heighten your understanding and experience of this book.

An extraordinary future is yours for the taking, and together we will unlock and activate the pathway to the door to your best life by paying more attention to who you are than to what you do. I'll show you how to take responsibility for the circumstances in your life, which will free you to be yourself — something that also leads to extraordinary outer changes in your world.

As you evolve, your life improves.

And as a result, your interest in step-by-step goals with their linear emphasis on getting this or that, will start to fall by the wayside; in their stead, you will develop an understanding of what coaching does: it enables you to create the conditions in your world so that great things can find you. As you read this book, I'd like you to imagine that we are working on an archaeological dig. With me as your LYBL Coach, we will brush away the deep-set mud and dust from your life in order to allow its outline to appear, your very own blueprint for your best life to come to the surface.

And it will.

# PREPARE TO DIG:

# HOW YOU WILL CREATE YOUR'LIVE YOUR BEST LIFE™' BLUEPRINT

This book will take you through 3 stages of your best life blueprint creation, which I have affectionately named:

- YOUR AWAKENING
- YOUR ACTIONS
- YOUR BEING

Much like any archaeological dig, the bones and other findings (YOUR AWAKENING) are only the beginning.

The other stages serve to put the bones together and allow what was supposed to be, and once was, to be again.

## YOUR AWAKENING

*Your Awakening* is a very necessary first stage. It assists you to bring forth the more productive thinking that will get you what you truly desire.

## YOUR ACTIONS

*Your Actions* will aid you in understanding the physical actions you need to take in order to create the life circumstances and changes that breed your very own version of your best life. This is where you obtain your sense of satisfaction, success and fulfilment towards all you do.

## YOUR BEING

*Your Being* introduces you to you, the real you, your best you. It also provides you with your best life elixir; opening up your life to the real magic you always knew was there. It will guide you to stretch so that you can tap into your own spiritual resources that will assist you to set up your life to receive the unexpected.

This stage will allow you to recognise your own signs in your innate wisdom that are trying to guide you, and allow you to notice that they were always there, you simply had to know how to access them.

# YOUR 10 "LIVE YOUR BEST LIFE™" STRATEGIES

As your move through the three stages, you'll work through ten strategies that are encapsulated throughout the chapters of this book:

1. **Know Your 'Why' & then ask Yourself 'What'** — in this first strategy, you will learn the essential questions that will guide and inspire you to begin to move forward. These questions are at the core of my coaching success with clients and without them I have found people simply stay stuck where they are.

2. **Acknowledge Your Current Beliefs & Reprogram You're Thinking** – in this strategy you will learn ways in which to recognise and acknowledge your current limiting and 'negative' beliefs and to start laying new foundations that empower you. As you begin to understand new ways to reprogram your current thinking, you will in essence hold the keys needed to unlock you from all that has been holding you back until now.

3. **Develop a Healthy Perspective** – there's perspective and then there is healthy perspective. Let's work together through this chapter to ensure you gain the clarity you need to in order to gain a clearer, more healthy perspective on yourself which will enable you to move through work, day to day and life challenges more quickly and more fluidly, with grace and ease.

4. **Listen to Your Feelings & Allow them to Guide You** - this strategy will enable you to learn to act on what you feel and not on what you think. In this strategy we will

explore ways in which you are able to transition from thinking to action by allowing your feelings to guide you.

5. **Create Your Own Personal Manifesto** – Imagine how empowering it feels as you begin to language and understand what you need to do to have every part of your life working in alignment. This strategy will allow you to get off the treadmill you have found yourself on and free you from trading your own time to your own present circumstances. Learn to state things how you would like them to be and allow them to flow to you.

6. *Discover & Reveal Your Own Self Worth* – As you understand and begin to be open to receiving all the hidden messages in your dreams and aspirations, you will soon also discover your own self-worth, which will lead you to exposing your lucrative purpose that's currently woven within them. This strategy will hold the clues that enable you to tap into this both financially and in terms of your greater richness and all you have to offer this world.

7. *Unleash Your Magnetic Super Powers* – Welcome to your magnetic super powers. This is where you start to accept that you knew you were always a super hero, you simply needed to step into being your own superhero and commence to wield your very own super powers. As with all magnets, there will be conditions that repel or attract more resourceful things to you. So in this strategy we explore how to unleash your magnetic powers in a way that truly benefits you.

8. ***Become a Master of Focus & Being*** – The key ingredient to seeing your best life recipe really starting to take shape. At this stage, you will make the transition from action to its best-life buddy and partners called 'FOCUS' and 'BEING'. Being present in each and every moment so that you experience the power of now. This is where you will see and feel your life has changed.

9. ***Ask For Directions Before You Set Out*** – In this strategy you will be presented with simple solutions that allow you to easily tap into and listen to your intuition. As you do this you will notice how smart it really is, and you will notice how it also has your best interests at heart. As you allow it to direct you moving forward you will learn to depend on it for guidance and as a result you will find fulfilling solutions to your life queries simply waiting there to direct you forward.

10. ***Embrace Your Uncertainty*** – In this final strategy you will give up your need to be certain of an outcome before you take any action. Now that you have tapped into your intuition, you will be able to trust what it is telling you. You will now find ways to take action, follow through and achieve outcomes purely based on your desires and what you are feeling and not what you think you should be doing.

For you to achieve the maximum impact and results from these strategies, I suggest you work through all of these strategies in order. There is logic to their sequence and they have been designed that way so the journey towards your best life will unfold, as it should. If, however, you do decide to jump around out of the suggested order or focus on only one or two strategies, there really is no right or wrong, so they will still work for you.

If at any stage you do begin to feel lost or stuck, I suggest that you go back to earlier steps and re-engage with the strategies that caused you the most challenge, as that is where your gap will be, and where you will need to stretch in order to grow.

For example, if you find yourself in the 'Your Actions' section working on your personal manifesto, and you cannot 'get over' blaming what is wrong or focusing on what is missing or lacking in your life, you will then need to revisit the 'Your Awakening' section and engage in those coaching exercises again.

If any element on your path to you discovering and exploring ways to your best life causes you deep emotional upheaval or upset, please do find the support you need. Coaching is a great means by which to acknowledge the past and how it served us, thank it and then give it new meaning. As we do this we find ways in which to focus on and design the future. If your past is a problem for you today then please nurture you. Make it a priority and take care of it so that you can move forward.

By the same token, you may find you're more comfortable in one of the three stages more than the others. For example, those who are highly analytical, skilled at unraveling complicated situations, and perhaps need to justify or have answers for everything are likely to relate very naturally to the 'Your Awakening'.

If you are immersed in a world of global pursuits, travelling here and there, negotiating and shaking on deals, working non-stop, and you still feel dissatisfied, you are probably innately well versed in the 'Your Actions' - the doing. Working like crazy, doing a lot of stuff, feeling like you are spinning your wheels in mud, yet not really getting anywhere. And if you are here, then I know, you are already feeling very tired and are desperately wishing for the world to stop so you can get off for a while.

Like my client Anita, whom you'll read about in Part Two, you will begin to discover how to make your life function again; it may be tiring, stressful and somewhat out of balance right now, but there is a way and you will find it.

On the other hand if you have a hard time making concrete parts of your life work, and gaining some good solid traction, you may be already very spiritually developed and open to 'Your Being'; even the most enlightened beings can have financial challenges if they have not gained or tapped into their worldly wisdom too.

Working across all three stages, not just the one in which you are most comfortable, is the key to discovering your very own blueprint, your peace of mind and ease of accomplishment.

Although I am coaching you through this book, you may also wish to develop a live coaching relationship with a professional coach or by teaming up with a partner, friend or small group to get the most out of your learning as you develop your way forward. Articulating your desires will bring them towards you.

# ACKNOWLEDGING & ACCESSING YOUR WISDOM

I believe that the idea of 'gaining' wisdom is a bit of a misnomer. As I see it, wisdom is the memory of the soul. It is the source of the meaning we have given things, the beliefs we have formed due to experience, the purpose and satisfaction that so many of us are waiting for. We don't so much gain wisdom as we lose along the way what wisdom we were born with. It then becomes our task to uncover it underneath all the cultural and experiential baggage that has kept us from finding it.

When you use this book well, you will start to recognise truths that you know but had forgotten, as well as lessons that you didn't even realise until now that you had learnt. You'll drop the habits that have kept you from hearing the internal promptings that have the power to positively guide the course of your life. You'll gain the tools to bring to the surface the things you already deeply know and the courage to put these insights into action.

As we journey together through these three stages towards living your best life, I will give you the following tools to assist you on your dig.

They will include:

### LYBL Questions:
When you use 'LYBL QUESTIONS' you will begin the process of living your best life. You will move from 'why' questions which ask for a reason, to 'what' questions, moving you to a place of self-empowerment. In these first stages of your discovery they will enable you to examine what is 'wrong' or 'missing' in your life and then pinpoint ways to solve your problems. You'll be asked to use these kinds of questions throughout

this book. These are the power questions that most coaches will engage to tap into the source of the matter with any client.

## LYBL in Action/s:

These exercises will help you crystallise what you are learning during each of the three stages of discovering your best life. They will have the most impact if performed right when you first read them; however, if you choose to return to the exercises later, that is fine too. The important thing is to do them, because coaching works from the actions you take, not just the awareness you gain. You may want to practice 'LYBL in Action' exercises a number of times in areas of this program, especially in those moments where you may feel stuck.

## LYBL through Writing:

As we journey together, there will be times I'll ask you to find out more about yourself by writing. Writing is a great way to move you from what you have grown accustomed to in your ordinary world, a world where you spend a lot of time consumed in your thoughts. There is so much power in the written and spoken word, because once you articulate something, you can then really start to own it. If you can state it, then you can have it, it can be yours. 'LYBL through Writing' allows you to access your own wisdom, which may have been hiding in the corners and crevices of your highly analytical mind, or in that part of your mind that fell asleep with your dreams many years ago. It's time for you to wake it up and allow it to tell you what it already knows.

## Your LYBL Journal:

Your 'LYBL Journal' that is offered in conjunction with this book will act as your companion guide, and will be the place you turn to for all the LYBL coaching exercises as we traverse the landscape of this book. I will prompt you throughout the course of this book when to grab it and use it. If you haven't already invested in your own LYBL Journal, then please create a personal journal of your own to assist your journey.

Your 'LYBL Journal' will be your sacred place of self-discovery, the journal that records every part of your archaeological dig in detail and also anything else that you discover or unearth along the way. Allow it to be your confidante and friend; that place where you know that no judgment resides. This will form a huge part of your excavation towards exposing your best life blueprint. Keep it handy, keep it with you, and love it as if you have been reunited with your first true love.

### LYBL Stories:

The experiences of many of my clients and workshop participants, along with my very own personal and life experiences will bring to life the work we are doing together. This book is designed to give you step-by-step work that produces immediate results. Change does happen in an instant. You may wish you had done it sooner, but don't waste any energy on regrets. Take your time, and you'll learn how to get from where you are to where you are meant to be - happily living your best life... because after all, wasn't that what you were born to do?

# PART ONE

# YOUR AWAKENING

*"Why are you knocking at every other door? Go knock at the door of your own heart."*

— *Rumi*

During the course of a normal day, we have about sixty-thousand thoughts, many of which come and go so quickly that we are not even aware of them. Some of these thoughts may set us up to 'win' in life. Yet how many of our thoughts keep us from engaging with our actual potential?

That is a question only you can answer, and each non-productive or unresourceful thought is an impediment to your personal fulfilment that only you can change.

I had never placed much value or authenticity in those motivational people who spruik positive thinking. Yet I learnt the value of their message as soon as I felt I had no other choice in my life but to change what I was thinking, one thought at a time, one old strategy at a time, in order to turn my life around. And it did, and that is something for which I most certainly give thanks to my Dad for exposing me to that from an early age.

Even today, I still get a little irritated at people who sound overly positive, because I know real life has its inevitable ebbs and flows, its ups and downs and I have learnt this through the greatest of my life's experiences. In my view it's a sign of maturity when a person can admit to having all the shades of emotions of human experience and be okay with that. There is something truly powerful when people truly own where they are at because it is only in that moment that we can face true acceptance of ourselves. Anything brushed aside or under the carpet will always re-appear.

With this in mind, and even though I can definitely see and understand the benefits, I am not going to throw the-power-of-positive-thinking rhetoric your way as I have since learnt better. What I will do however in the following chapters is walk you through very practical ways in which you can use your mind to access your best life blueprint more quickly in order to then lead you to your best life. I believe this to be more truthful and more sustainable for there is so much to be said for the power of vulnerability.

'Your Awakening' is the first stage in starting your dig, along with the reconstruction of some of your life's blueprint. To live up to the life you were meant to lead, you must begin by looking at what has blocked you, what has held you back and prevented you from hearing your own inner voice of wisdom. When you begin to awaken you are able to understand why you may be seeing the world in a less productive or less conducive way.

The main task of this stage is not to understand the influence the past has had on your life, but to give you the tools you need to move forward. The purpose of 'Your Awakening' is to assist you to 'get over yourself': You have to accept that you have what you have, you are what you are, your parents did what they did, and that you still deserve to lead and have an extraordinary life - to live your best life.

As you work through this first stage of uncovering your life's plan, you are making a commitment to overcoming the biggest obstacle to most people's attainment of satisfaction with their lives - themselves.

You are committing to overcoming negative self-concepts, limiting beliefs and habits that aren't serving you and that can get in the way of the wisdom and learnings that are trying to lead you to your best life.

In the next three chapters, you will learn how to get over these hurdles by asking better questions in order to get better answers to your life's queries, reframing beliefs that stunt your ability to have what you want and gaining the perspective to allow your life's desires to take flight.

There are many ways in which 'Your Awakening' will arrive. Let's take a look at a client of mine named Christopher, and as we do, it will assist you to gain an understanding as to how 'Your Awakening' is an essential part of your journey.

Christopher desperately wanted for his company to reach the top of its game within is chosen market of recruitment in the mining industry.

His naturally volatile temperament, combined with his fierce determination to make this happen, was working against him.

When we began to work together, I told him that if success was indeed part of his ultimate life plan, some awakening was needed. He needed to get out of his own way and change the questions he posed.

Instead of "Who is responsible for this?", "How dare you speak to me that way", or "Who does he think he is?", he needed to be asking, "What do I want from this situation?", "What would be the best outcome?", "What would be fair to everyone?" and "What will make the difference for us to be the most respected in our field?"

Christopher had to gain perspective and realise that not everything that was happening around him was actually about him. He needed to adjust some of his beliefs that he held about his own self worth and the value he can add and how to prove it.

Once he did this, he was free of the struggle. He decided to create a way forward for his entire company that did not compromise his newfound clarity.

What moved Christopher from being purely reactive to his work to being on track with his best life blueprint is what we will explore for you in 'Your Awakening'.

Even if you don't think you have any awakening to do, it is even more essential for you to work through this part. The exercises in the three chapters that follow will benefit you regardless of whether you think you need them.

So, let's get started :)

# CHAPTER 1

# KNOW YOUR 'WHY' & THEN
# ASK YOURSELF 'WHAT'?

**N**ow is the time to connect with your mind.

Time to free up your capacity for new learnings, and allow this chapter to deliver them to you in the most efficient way.

This chapter is all about connecting you to the first powerful tool that you need in order to access the inner wisdom I speak of, because as you do so, this new learning will quite literally change your life.          ·

Now, don't go freaking out on me in this first chapter, when I share with you this everyday, very ordinary, yet very powerful tool.

Do you promise? Are we all cool?

The most powerful tool you have, you already know.

It is the power of the common question.

And I am sure you would agree with me, when I say, that one of the most common questions we ask is 'WHY?' 'Why' it would seem is the language we all use when we are seeking to understand.

When we were young children, we used to ask this question to figure out how the world works: "Why is the sky blue?", "Why did Lamby (my pet lamb) run away?" And as we get older, we still use 'why' to bring our circumstances into alignment within our ability to understand our world.

'Why' definitely has its powerful place in our lives, because without understanding the purpose behind why we should do something we may as well not do it at all.

However, I have found that 'why' can eventually lose its power to move us forward. Instead of using it in its most powerful form, we tend to get 'stuck' by obsessing over questions like, "Why did that happen?", "Why am I this way?", "Why did this happen to me?", "Why aren't I better-thinner-smarter?"

Even if you're not in the pits of despair or survival, you might still be stuck using victim or despair questions. When you use 'Why' to ask a question, you are struggling to come up with the information to help you understand a situation or a circumstance and in most circumstances even the information presented can be flawed as it will always relate to your perception of your own reality and not necessarily what took place.

I call this asking an 'information question'. Information questions will give you answers that explain the past. They present answers that fill the corners of your mind with details, as well as emotion, blame, and perhaps even more problems.

While you can assume that obtaining more information will enable you to be released from your problems, an information question does little to move you forward in life. In fact, sometimes they can't even be answered.

In working with clients, now for just over three decades, I've seen them endure more frustration than necessary because they asked too many information questions and I have since learnt that there is actually such a thing as a bad question contrary to all the sayings out there.

Now, don't go getting me all wrong here, when it comes to connecting us to our overarching life's purpose we definitely need to understand the big 'WHY' behind it, because if we don't then we quite simply won't be linking any action we take towards the outcome we truly desire. Asking 'WHY' has definitely been the key to many a brilliant self-discovery story, however, when it comes to creating and making the change you need to make, 'why' is not an effective short-term tool. You need to understand 'why', but also understand that it is not going to be the answer towards what happens next.

The way to your best life blueprint requires asking deeper, more useful questions in order to get better answers and more effective action. The questions that will help you do that are what I call 'access questions', which I also like to call 'LYBL QUESTIONS'.

'LYBL QUESTIONS' access your innate wisdom, the wisdom with which you were born, to create positive forward motion, reminding all of us how resourceful we are and that we already have all we need within us. We simply forget it at times. So this is here to serve as a reminder and to put you back in the driver's seat.

# LYBL QUESTIONS

Imagine your brain as one big 'Google Machine'. It is a search engine tapping into a database of information just like the World Wide Web that you already have available to you and that is made up of acquired experience, knowledge and intuition. When you need answers in life, you form questions that serve as your key words. Your brain then searches its resources and gives out all the possible answers. The more specific your keyword entry, the more specific your answers - that's the wisdom of your very own internal built computer. How did it know what you needed exactly? You told it your question and it found the answer for you. With that point alone, I need you to stop and take notice.

This is what 'LYBL QUESTIONS' will do - assist you to be specific in your information gathering so you can come up with the answers that have the power to move you forward.

Nearly all the questions we are used to begin with one of five words: 'who', 'what', 'why', 'when' or 'how'. And although these words assist us to gather facts and understand each other in conversation, not all of them exude wisdom. Since we've already eliminated 'why' as a viable 'LYBL QUESTION', 'Who', 'When' and 'How' fall into the information question category.

Therefore we are left with using 'what' which aids the brain to behave as a more efficient search engine. 'What' questions force you to be specific in your query and being specific leads to solution and awareness; on the other hand, asking "Why?" leaves you with only the question.

For example, if I asked you, "Why are you reading this book?" you might tell me a story about some things you are wondering about. Maybe you'd go on to provide a few details about what brought you to this moment of information seeking. Your responses would probably have something to do with your past. But if I asked, "What outcome do you want to reach by reading this book?" the answer you give would be future-oriented. It would also be much more specific, since you would be forced to look forward, rather than backward. This releases energy and moves you from feeling stuck to living in possibility - you can see opportunities out into the horizon and into the future.

This is where the path to your best life commences. As you start to move toward what it is you do want, everything you are running from will lose its power.

So let me ask you that again: What outcome are you looking for by reading this book? Answers like "To live my best life", "To feel and be much happier in all that I do" or "To find the guts and courage to take a leap of faith" would be more like it - regardless of what the final result ends up being, these types of responses get you moving toward your desired outcome. And the best part is that they set the person up to feel empowered to achieve that momentum on their own.

The search engine in our brains is highly sophisticated and just like Google, it requires a well-phrased question to take advantage of it. When a question is phrased well, it gets us closer to the outcome, so when we take the time to consider what the 'Google Machine' needs, we have more opportunity to land more precisely with what it was we desired. So start Googling I say! Google yourself as much as you possibly can, by asking yourself the right questions in which to find the answers.

This is exactly why I use 'LYBL QUESTIONS', because they are designed to do just that. By using 'what' questions, you start accessing your own inner wisdom that you were born with, that already knows what it needs to know to guide you through.

The list below is a collection of powerful questions that are used by many coaches all around the world.

Take a look at the list of questions below and see how you can make any question an 'LYBL QUESTION' by using 'what'.

| 'LYBL' QUESTIONS | |
| --- | --- |
| Converting Information Questions into 'LYBL' Questions | |
| *Instead of asking yourself:* | *Ask:* |
| Why is this happening to me? | What do I need to get through this? |
| Why am I such a failure? | What will get me what I want? |
| Why aren't I better at this? | What can I do to improve? |
| Why can't I have a blessed life like 'such and such'? | What can I learn from 'such and such'? |
| Why can't I get it? | What do I need to understand? |

| Instead of asking others: | Ask: |
|---|---|
| Why did she say that? | What could have made her say that? |
| Whose fault is it? | What is the solution? |
| Who did what? | What would have made a difference? |
| What happened [seeking details] | What happened? [seeking outcome] |
| Why would they do that? | What could be learnt from this? |
| How will you do that? | What will you do? |

# HOW & WHEN TO USE 'LYBL QUESTIONS'?

Imagine 2 friends conversing and empathising over a problem.

One is expressing a complaint and the other is taking the supportive role.

If the supporter was to ask information questions – "Where were you?", "Who started it?", "Why?", they would be treated to details about who did what to whom in a blow-by-blow re-enactment of the drama.

However, if the supporter knew how to ask 'LYBL QUESTIONS', "What is upsetting about what happened?", the friend with the problem would move from problem to solution in record-breaking time.

And that I believe is the key here.

For you to be able to move from 'problem' to 'solution' as quickly and resourcefully as possible.

So that you can find the appropriate 'what' questions to ask, you must change the focus from the details and information and bring to light the desired outcomes, potential outcomes and all the areas of possibility.

Move away from trying to understand a problem and move toward solving it. In the process, you'll see that you don't really need to understand the dilemma to know how to solve it. Using 'what' questions will train you to think towards the future, as if you are already ahead of the problem.

'What' assumes that a solution is the goal, to the exclusion of everything else. It always finds a way.

Sometimes, we want to be left alone with our problems for a while.

Have you ever tried to help a friend who didn't really want help?

Remember how frustrated that left you feeling? When you or someone you know wants to continually keep reflecting on a problem over and over again, with no real desire to solve it, in this instance, all the 'LYBL QUESTIONS' in the world are not going to help. You must truly want to stop the record from spinning round and round in circles and desire for the problem to be solved if 'what' questions are to have their desired outcome and effect.

Even though you can do this by yourself, I believe it is really powerful to play witness and be a part of seeing other people gain clarity when you ask them 'what' questions.

Asking 'LYBL QUESTIONS' is a productive and highly generous listening tool for you to use with friends, colleagues and loved ones. Allowing another person to hear themselves is a wonderful gift. This kind of thoughtful communication takes time and patience to master, and as you do so, you will find that it deeply improves the quality of all your relationships.

So, whether you use 'LYBL QUESTIONS' to move yourself or someone else forward, keep in mind that you now have a great, simple and efficient tool.

All these reasons mentioned above are why I choose to use 'LYBL QUESTIONS' with my clients. It truly enables them to create more positive circumstances and to move toward their outcomes more quickly than they do on their own. These questions alone predictably set clients up for both small and large breakthroughs. The best part is that it is my clients who already have the answers within them; I am simply there asking the right questions, prompting them in order to accelerate their own self-discovery mission.

Nothing makes me happier than when I hear a client say, "That's a good question." Or better yet, "I hate you for asking me that!". Those are surefire signs that we have struck pure gold – the gold that I call their innate wisdom. These are the boundary conditions that you know need to be crossed in order to have them explore new territory. I call it the territory of possibility. This is where anything becomes possible.

Now that you are ready to start using 'LYBL QUESTIONS', let's get question asking to work for you.

Don't focus too much on the need to be right, simply run off the principles of asking 'what' instead of 'why'. As with everything, the more you do it the more familiar it will become.

Below you will see two conversations that cover the same subject matter, yet with dramatically different results.

In the first conversation, you'll see a coach speak with a client in a more conventional way, WITHOUT using 'LYBL QUESTIONS'.

| 'LYBL' QUESTIONS | |
|---|---|
| **Coach & Client Interaction WITHOUT using LYBL Questions** | |
| **CLIENT:** | Something's really bothering me about this decision and I can't quite put my finger on it. |
| **COACH:** | Why do you think that is? |
| **CLIENT:** | I don't know. I've been giving it a lot of thought, but nothing seems to stand out. |
| **COACH:** | Why do you think this is bothering you? |
| **CLIENT:** | It's just something about him that I don't trust |
| **COACH:** | Was it something he said to you? |

| CLIENT: | Oh, he said he knew these people who could help me to get it sorted, when I asked who they were, he avoided giving me names. |
| COACH: | How did that make you feel? |
| CLIENT: | Annoyed. |
| COACH: | Did any one thing particularly annoy you? |
| CLIENT: | Just everything. |
| COACH: | Do you know what you want to do now? |
| CLIENT: | I think I just want to drop the whole thing and walk away. But I'm just not sure. |

The Coach's questions asked here focus on information seeking, and in such a non-specific way that the client isn't prompted to provide dynamic answers that would propel them forward. There is no freedom from the problem, no break from its burden, no movement toward a solution.

And from my experience, this is how most interactions play out! No wonder people feel stuck and frustrated!

Now compare the approach in this next example, where the Coach uses 'LYBL QUESTIONS'.

| 'LYBL' QUESTIONS | |
| --- | --- |
| **Coach & Client Interaction <u>WITH</u> using LYBL Questions** | |
| CLIENT: | Something's really bothering me about this decision and I can't quite put my finger on it. |
| COACH: | Take a guess – *what* is it that you feel is bugging you? |

| CLIENT: | I don't know. |
|---------|---------------|
| COACH: | *What* if you did know? *What* if you pretended you knew, *what* would you say? |
| CLIENT: | Hmm. I don't trust the guy who brought me the idea. |
| COACH: | You don't trust the guy. *What* led you to that conclusion? |
| CLIENT: | He has been very vague. He won't commit to anything he has said. I've even been asking him about it. |
| COACH: | *What* do you need to move ahead? |
| CLIENT: | I need to find someone I can trust. |
| COACH: | Great. Any ideas as to who? |
| CLIENT: | Yes. There's another guy I think could do the job much better |
| COACH: | When will you call him? |
| CLIENT: | Today! |

Now we're talking…..clarity, relief, action, and a way forward.

Here, the client's answers are dynamic, empowering and they ring with certainty.

Wisdom is attained and, with it, a break from the burden of the problem.

This liberating break is the result of using 'LYBL QUESTIONS'.

# IT'S TIME TO GRAB YOUR 'LYBL' JOURNAL!

## 'LYBL' IN ACTION

### Using 'LYBL' Questions

It's now time for you to practice what you've learned.

Spend the next 24 hours using 'LYBL QUESTIONS' on your career and in your life.

Instead of telling someone what to do, ask him or her a question.

Before jumping in to deal with a problem or a challenge with a team member, ask them "What do you see that we can do here?".

If your best friend is frustrated and feeling stuck because all they can see is problems everywhere, ask her, "What do you want to see happen in this situation?". If she can answer, then ask another question: "What's the first step you need to take?".

Keep asking questions until the person you're dealing with comes up with their own solution/s.

Make it clear from the outset of any such conversation that you are trying out something new on them. Keep your tone light and fun, asking, "Do you mind if I ask you some questions, to see if I can assist you to come up with a solution to your problem?"

Here is an extensive list of 'LYBL QUESTIONS'.

It may assist you to have this list in front of you when you do this activity so that you can use it as a guide.

What do you want?
What are you afraid of?
What is this costing you?
What are you attached to?
What is the dream?
What is the essence of the dream?
What is beyond this problem?
What is ahead?
What are you building toward?
What has happened for you to feel successful?
What gift are you not being responsible for?
What are your healthy sources of energy?

What's stopping you?
What's in your way?
What would make the biggest difference?
What do you like to do?
What can you do to make you happy right now?
What do you hope to accomplish by having that conversation?
What do you hope to accomplish by doing that?
What's the first step?
What would it be like to experience the excitement and fear at the same time?
What's important about this?
What would it take for you to treat yourself like your best client?
What benefit / payoff is there in the present situation?
What do you expect to happen?
What's the ideal?
What's the ideal outcome?
What would it look like?
What's the truth?
What's the right action?
What are you going to do?
What's working for you?
What would you do differently?
What decision would you make from a position of strength?
What other choices do you have available to you?
What do you really, really want?
What if there were no limits?
What haven't I asked that I should ask?

What needs to be said that has not been said?

What are you not saying?

What else do you have to say about that?

What is left to do to have this be complete?

What do you have invested in continuing to do it this way?

What is that?

What comes first?

What consequence are you avoiding?

What is the value you have received from this conversation?

What is motivating / inspiring you?

What has you hooked?

What is missing here?

What does that remind you of?

What do you suggest?

What is underneath that?

What is this person contributing to the quality of your life?

What is it that you are denying yourself right now?

What do you need to put in place to accomplish this?

What is the simplest solution here?

What would help you know I support this/you completely?

What happened?

What are you avoiding?

What is the worst that could happen?

What are you committed to?

What is your vision for yourself and the people around you?

What don't you want?
What if you did know?
What's your heart telling you?
What are you willing to give up?
What might you have done differently?
What are you not facing?
What does this feeling remind you of?
What would you do differently if you tapped into your own wisdom?
What does your soul say?

. . . . . . . . . . . . . . . . . . . . . . . . . . . . . . . . .

Over the next 24 hours use your LYBL Journal to record your experiences.

Were some conversations better than others?

Which ones, and why?

Also jot down how you might incorporate 'LYBL QUES-TIONS' into your life more now that you have experience with them.

# ALLOW 'WHAT' TO ACCESS THE WISDOM YOU WERE BORN WITH

## 'LYBL' STORY: ENTER PENNY

$P$enny is a corporate executive who participated in one of my 'Live Your Best Life' seminars. She told me about a team member who always saw the glass half empty, never half full. He would find the fault in anything and the negative side of everything. Penny felt he didn't want to take responsibility for his actions. He justified everything he did by saying it was someone else's fault or someone gave him the wrong information.

Penny struggled with how to get him to see that he was indeed involved and accountable for his own words and actions.

On a recent conference call, Penny had to deliver some difficult news to her team about significant changes in the company. This team member was on the call and was disruptive and very self-involved. It made her realise she had to address his behaviour sooner rather than later.

"What I really wanted to say to him," Penny told me, "Was 'Who' do you think you are? Why do you expect me or the company to help you? Why do you always see things in the most negative light? If you spent less time on the phone gossiping, you'd have the time and positive energy to devote to planning and executing for success. And the way to get any positive reinforcement from me, or to get me to embrace the issue as you see it, is not by being passive-aggressive on a conference call, asking me the same question four times, or pushing my hot buttons in an attempt to corner me into a response. Whether you like it or not, I am the manager. You are the contractor. This is not a democracy, I will lead and you will follow."

Instead, Penny addressed the issue with her team member in a casual conversation over dinner. She had her notes from my seminar with her, along with a list of 'LYBL QUESTIONS'. Here's what she said:

"On our conference call, I picked up on the tension in your voice. Tell me what you found upsetting about the new incentive plan. Let me ask that another way. What emotion was triggered in you as we discussed the plan? What do you want now? What is your goal for the year? What will get you what you want? What can I do to help? What can we do together to make it work?"

The team member was blown away, yet also felt stopped in his tracks. He'd been expecting Penny to go for the jugular, but she didn't buy into his crisis. She consciously decided to pull back and once he realised there would be no fight, he was forced to respond in the same way. The 'LYBL QUESTIONS' Penny asked left no room for excuses, self-justification, or any defensive behaviour. He was left with no-one to look at but himself. After this frank, open discussion, he and Penny were aware of his insecurities, his fears and his goals.

She was able to learn what he wanted from her as his manager because she used 'LYBL QUESTIONS'. They diffused a very difficult situation. You saw the raw emotional reaction in her words to me, which anyone could understand and relate to.

However, Penny made a deliberate choice to seek a solution instead of fishing for more information, and getting mired in emotion, blame and details. In doing so, she was able to improve a working relationship that she long ago decided was beyond repair. This was a challenge for Penny, but in committing to elevating the exchange, she challenged her co-worker too, and together they got new, unexpected results.

'LYBL QUESTIONS' were essential in making this possible.

## 'LYBL QUESTIONS' AND YOUR RELATIONSHIPS

You've seen how 'LYBL QUESTIONS' help in a work-related scenario, yet they are equally effective in other areas of your life, such as romantic relationships.

My friend Trevor recently told me how 'LYBL QUESTIONS' led him and his wife to have what he said was "one of the best conversations", they'd had in years.

His wife had a problem she wanted to discuss, and what Trevor had done was resist his natural urge to jump in with a solution. Instead, he talked through the issues involved, using 'what' questions only.

His wife was able to solve her own problem, thanks in no small part to Trevor's attentive questions. She felt connected to him and very loved and supported.

Trevor understood that he did not have to 'do' anything for his wife. Nor did he have to 'fix' anything for her. Just asking the right questions was the loving, listening and helpful support she needed.

Doing this for someone I believe is the ultimate form of love. This allows people to move from a place of being rescued to a greater sense of personal power and feeling self-empowered. Empowerment is the ultimate stepping-stone to sustainability, which I believe is ecology that people truly desire in any intimate relationship.

Never underestimate the power of a few 'LYBL QUESTIONS' to raise the level of intimacy in a relationship. When people feel heard and when they are helped to hear themselves, they often experience a deep connection to the power they have. This is often translated into deep gratitude for the person who helped them get there. Whether they are conscious of it or not, this greater sense of connection to oneself and another makes for the kind of relationships most people are looking for.

I know this works wonders between my husband and myself.

## AN 'LYBL' CAUTION!!!!

As you begin to realise the benefit of using 'LYBL QUESTIONS' in your own home and work life, I need to warn you of an exception to the "It's good to ask 'What?'" rule.

There is in fact one 'what' question that is not an 'LYBL QUESTION', but an 'information' question. You've probably used it countless times on yourself and on others.

Are you ready for it?

It is…

"What should I do?"

Oh yes, that's a very big 'what' question, but definitely not an 'LYBL QUESTION'.

How many times have you asked your friends, "What should I do?" or told yourself you "really should" do x, y or z? The answers to "What should I do?" prevent you from asking the most powerful 'LYBL QUESTION' you can use.

It's very simple and it's the exact opposite:

"What do I want?"

That's it.

I know it sounds very simple. And yes, very easy.

Most people however have a really hard time answering this question, because most of us don't know what we want. I see this up close and personal everyday. Most smart, sophisticated people, with goals and plans, think they know what they want. However, truly having a sense of what would make them happy is a different story. We tend to be much more certain of what we should do, say, wear, or look like than of what will guide us to inner happiness.

In fact, most people do more to avoid pain than to gain pleasure.

It is my experience that seven out of ten people don't really know what they want.

They think they do, but they come to discover that much of what drives them is unmet needs or the expectations of others. We will work on making sure you do know what you want in Part Two of this book, so for now avoid asking the information question "What should I do?" and replace it instead with "What do I want?"

# IT'S TIME TO GRAB YOUR 'LYBL' JOURNAL!

## 'LYBL' IN ACTION

### What Do I Want?

Start making it a habit to ask yourself, before every conversation, every decision and every meeting, "What do I want?"

For example, if you are about to make a call that makes you anxious, take a minute to figure out what you want to have when that call ends. A job, a sale, an apology, an agreement to revisit the topic if the opportunity arises?

If you can't answer, take a deep breath and ask again. If the answer still eludes you, explore whether you really want something at all or if you are just reacting to something you've left unsaid or are feeling needy in some way.

Maybe you really want to finish the argument in a way that feels better or get a raise without having to plead for it. Maybe what you really want is something as simple as a hug. An actor would never walk on stage without knowing why his character is in the scene.

By asking, "What do I want?" you too will know what you have come to accomplish.

# 'LYBL STORY': ENTER BRENDA

### WHAT IS MORE POWERFUL: 'WANT' OR 'SHOULD'?

$M$y phone rang. It was time for Brenda's third session with me and, upon picking up the phone, I could instantly hear agitation. "I've been trying to rewrite my CV all week and I just can't decide which direction will make it what I want it to be. Should I be focusing on getting a job in advertising or make it read stronger for work in software marketing?"

Brenda was a singer / songwriter by avocation and a successful communications professional in the 'real world'. She wanted to solidify her plans to find more fulfilling work in the career that paid the bills and, at the same time, further her artistic endeavours.

In our earlier sessions, she had said things like "I just don't know what to do. I have to think more about what I should do. Maybe if I try to do both. What do you think I should do?"

"What I think doesn't matter right now," I'd replied. "What you think does."

Brenda's high level of anxiety and her constant use of the word 'should' was a red flag, so I gave her an assignment. "Brenda," I said, "for the next week, I want you to eliminate the word 'should' from your vocabulary."

After a moment of silence, Brenda asked, "Well, what should I say?". She then had a laugh to herself, realising that the 'S' word had slipped out again.

"Use the word 'want' for one week and see what happens. Ask yourself what you want instead of repeatedly asking what you should do."

When we had our next session on the phone, it was like I was speaking to a new person.

"Hi Brenda."

"Hi Michele. I want to be in advertising!"

By asking herself 'LYBL QUESTIONS' instead of information seeking "What should I do?" Brenda was able to discover what she truly wanted. She had carved wisdom out of all her confusion simply by changing the questions she was asking. She was starting to unlock the life that would make her happiest.

# SET YOUR INTENTION & LOOK BEYOND THE WORDS

We have seen that changing a few words in a 'LYBL QUES-TION' can make a world of difference in the quality of the answer you receive, and the truth is that changing the words alone is not enough. Going from good to great answers to 'LYBL QUESTIONS' depends not only on what words you use but also on where your underlying focus is. Everything must start out with the right intention.

To get the most productive results, your underlying focus should be on solutions and forward motion for your life. When you play with the words, the questions change and their power to change your life multiply. By committing to monitoring your inner motivation, however, you not only change your life, but you begin to transform who you are.

When you can remain grounded and stay focused on solutions and forward motion during the adversities of your life, you've already begun to align with your blueprint.

Your life can flow instead of getting stopped behind a dam of blame, criticism, problems and anxiety. The focus on your inner motivation (intention) makes all the difference.

In 'Your Awakening' there are really only two choices: are you someone who intends to stay 'stuck', or are you someone who intends to move forward?

To use 'LYBL QUESTIONS' successfully, you must intend to move forward.

To live well you must never stop moving forward.

I'm not talking about motion for motion's sake; it's more about focusing your efforts on getting out of any potholes as soon as you can, even if you fall back into them later. Although such a shift in focus may require a fundamental change in you, it's the only way to ensure that when you ask 'LYBL QUESTIONS', you're not just mouthing the words.

# ARE YOU SEEKING INFORMATION OR ARE YOU SEEKING WISDOM?

Let's take a look at the kinds of intentions you've been working with.

The following list describes two very different kinds of motivation in asking questions.

Most people are basically either seeking information or they are seeking wisdom, although you may exhibit characteristics of both.

Which type are you?

# IT'S TIME TO GRAB YOUR 'LYBL' JOURNAL!

| LYBL IN ACTION | |
|---|---|
| **Seeking Information or Seeking Wisdom** | |
| *Characteristics of an Information Seeker* | *Characteristics of a Wisdom Seeker* |
| Ask questions that are self-centred or self fulfilling (What's wrong with me, the world, the situation in relation to how it affects me?) | Asks questions that are focused outward (What's right about me, the world, and the situation? How does it add up to a whole?) |
| Digs for evidence to justify point of view | Explores as an objective observer to find truth |
| Is oriented toward problems | Is oriented toward solutions |
| Is territorial and assumes everything is scarce | Assumes ample resources are available |
| Hoards and controls information and knowledge | Sees information and knowledge as things to be shared |
| Reacts without thinking to problems and people | Thinks and reflects before taking action |

| Must have or give answers as part of identity | Is comfortable with waiting for answers and with appearing to 'not know' temporarily |
| Holds knowledge as a source of power, something to manipulate or control | Holds knowledge as a source of power, something to inspire and transform |

Each list will give you choices as to how you can use questions and assist you to determine which characteristics you are predisposed to. There is nothing wrong with finding yourself in the seeking of information list, however you will come to see that you can make better choices, ask different questions and produce less stressful outcomes if you focus on seeking more wisdom.

To experience your life unfolding with ease, the shift from information seeker to wisdom seeker becomes necessary.

We will explore how to make the shifts in Part Two and Three, but let's use the next coaching exercise to learn how your motivation may need to change.

Take your time here, in order to absorb how this could transform your life.

# IT'S TIME TO GRAB YOUR 'LYBL' JOURNAL!

## 'LYBL' THROUGH WRITING

### Applying 'LYBL Questions' to Real Life

Write down all the complaints or issues you are facing in your life right now.

Here's an example:

My girlfriend wants to buy a house, and I'm not ready. She keeps nagging me and we're both unhappy.

Then record all the frustrating and bewildering information questions that you have about these issues.

Why is this happening? Why can't she just understand that I'm not ready? How do I get her to drop the subject?

Now write down, as many 'LYBL QUESTIONS' as you can that are pertinent to the issue or issues.

What will make the difference in my relationship with my girlfriend? What needs to be said that I have not said? What can help us both get our needs met?

Notice the difference between your information questions and your 'LYBL QUESTIONS'.

The final step in this coaching exercise is to come up with an answer to every information question and every 'LYBL QUESTION' that you listed.

Notice the difference in the answers the two kind of questions brings.

Even though I've drilled it into your head that information questions don't move you forward, take the time to write out the answers to both kinds of questions so you can see how the inner motivation to move forward makes all the difference to this process.

Watch for action steps or clarity that may come from your 'LYBL QUESTIONS'.

Expect wisdom to flow.

You can even begin to take action where it is appropriate.

# COACHES WRAP UP

You have begun the excavation process that will lead to unearthing the blueprint to your best life. In this chapter, we learned these tips:

- Stop asking "WHY?"
- Ask 'LYBL QUESTIONS'
- Use "WHAT?" to access your innate wisdom
- Keep your attention on solutions and on the future
- Watch your motivation
- Focus on the characteristics of the wisdom seeker rather than the information    seeker in yourself

Keep these lessons handy as we continue to work. You may want to review them as you excavate your life blueprint.

# CHAPTER 2

# ACKNOWLEDGE YOUR CURRENT BELIEFS & THEN REPROGRAM YOUR THINKING

In the last chapter, you began to learn how to use 'LYBL QUESTIONS' instead of merely seeking information. In essence, what you were doing was training your brain to instinctively pursue your innate wisdom rather than taking the less productive route you've followed before. We spent time scratching your record, so that it is unable to play that old song over and over again.

In this chapter, you'll train your brain even further, in order to change your deepest thoughts into a course that will move you forward in your life.

That is what the 'Your Awakening' is all about.

In this next strategy, you will awaken further by disciplining yourself to use your thinking to its maximum benefit.

Up to this point, you may have been unconsciously confining your thoughts to negative assumptions about your life, and how life works in general. These assumptions may be stopping you from having what you really want. Let's take a look at how those beliefs determine the actions you are willing to take.

We'll explore how the possibility of changing a single thought can change the action we then take and therefore the result we get.

Just as you can train the muscles in your body to work more efficiently for your overall health, so can you train your brain to serve you better. Training your brain and reprogramming your thinking is a strategy that can bring you closer to unearthing your blueprint so that you can find your best life hidden deep within you.

# LIMITING BELIEFS

As I work with and guide people to assist them get what they want from their lives, I find that there are many unproductive thoughts and ruling ideas running around in people's minds, just like a rubbish tip, dumping rubbish here and there and as a result littering many a mind.

I call them 'limiting beliefs' since these ideas restrict and limit my clients' worlds.

Limiting beliefs are so deeply rooted in experience and so wonderfully steeped in evidence that they colour the lens through which you look at your entire life and the world itself. They permeate all of your thoughts, and influence what you say and what you do.

Limiting beliefs…they are boss.

After years of coaching others, it's become clear to me that limiting beliefs tend to be a much needed root of all-evil to allow growth and shift to occur. The relationship you can grow to understand between your limiting beliefs and how they play out in your world can also be the very thing that sets you free.

For you see, limiting beliefs tend to be the driving force behind not getting positive results in your life, and eventually as you start to awaken you will get to a point where enough is enough.

You will desire them to work for you rather than against you. For this to occur however, bringing awareness to them is essential.

My clients always seem to have the answers and they basically know what to do, so why aren't they doing it? In almost every case, taking positive action meant overcoming a fear or examining a long-held assumption.

Fears and assumptions are both limiting beliefs, thoughts that are so well integrated into your life that they feel right even though they may actually be wrong. Training and reprogramming the brain to give you the thought that both feels right and is right is what this strategy is all about.

Your brain contains truckloads and truckloads of rational thought; we spend our entire lives justifying the crap out of everything. And even though we spend most of our waking hours in this state, it is pertinent to also acknowledge the wisdom that is residing within us too.

However, just because you think something, doesn't mean it is true or that you should believe it.

We are so great at convincing ourselves of 'stuff' aren't we?

What I have learnt from experience is that the beliefs that deserve our time are the ones that fuel your imagination and your fullest self-expression. So, I say, believe in those thoughts that bring you to life, the ones that point you in the direction toward the best part of you, and kick those parts of you that are fearful and hung-up in the butt! Meet them head on, thank them for existing, which has allowed you to get to this point in your life, and then set them free.

So, how do you go about doing that I hear you ask?

Let me share with you here.

# EXPANDING BELIEFS

**B**ecause limiting beliefs tend to be fixed, or static, they also tend to keep you frozen in time, inactive or unsuccessful. They can significantly limit your potential if you allow them to, and especially if you leave them unrecognised. The good news is that as soon as you can recognise a limiting belief, it can be refocused to be an expanding belief, one that points to possibility like a spotlight and can launch you into a better future.

Your deeply held beliefs are what determine what you'll make of any situation. They are in essence how you view your world. Depending on whether they are limiting or expanding, you will find either possibility or you will encounter a roadblock.

# 'LYBL' STORY: ENTER MARY

**M**ary is a perfect example of someone whose thinking had prevented her from living her best life. She had a deeply held belief that was keeping her from leading the life she wanted. This limiting belief was the unfounded fear that if she allowed her small business to grow to where she truly hoped it would, she would lose her personal freedom, be tied to her desk inside her office forever; a never-ending chain of work-related responsibilities.

Losing her freedom was something she wanted to avoid at all costs - even that of her business's profitability. At the same time, Mary was greatly disappointed that her business had not developed and thrived as she'd envisioned.

Talk about being in conflict; two parts of her pulling her in totally different directions.

So there she sat before me, paralysed between two polar opposites - wanting freedom and wanting her business to take off – Mary was definitely feeling bruised and battered and was considering herself victimised and unlucky.

Mary had actually wondered if she would ever feel successful, so you can imagine all the limiting beliefs held up in that concept.

When Mary started coaching with me, our first area of focus was for her to recognise that her life was less than great, not because of some bad luck that had crept in to find her but because she was unknowingly, on an unconscious level taking only enough action to protect her limiting belief.

'Knowing' deep down that if the business succeeded, she would be 'robbed' or 'stripped' of her personal freedom, Mary had been unconsciously stopping herself from being more successful.

As we began to work together, she realised that success would only increase her freedom and her ability to pay for outside help if the workload became overwhelming.

I love these light bulb moments with clients and how they light up inside…I call them 'A-HA' moments. I have grown to thrive on those 'A-HA' moments that people create for themselves.

Once she had this 'A-HA' moment, her thinking changed and she began to see positive changes. Clients started to appear as if out of thin air. She developed a conviction that she could have a flourishing business and still have a life.

As her business began to grow, so did her newfound confidence.

Mary, now has a thriving business, but has set boundaries. By setting clear intentions of how she would like her life and business to be she is now no longer working on weekends and has dedicated evenings throughout the week where she works, no longer working late every night. She now feels empowered rather than stuck and bound by her business.

She has achieved her goals without losing anything. In essence, Mary retrained and reprogrammed her brain to move forward into the life she wanted. She turned a limitation into a possibility.

Time after time, I can point to example after example where just changing a thought, as Mary did, resulted in a shift to more positive circumstances.

Upon changing their thoughts from ones that always came to the conclusion a goal was 'impossible', to ones that insisted what they wanted for themselves was definitely possible, so many of my clients have reported that they are attracting new opportunities at a rapid rate of knots and the people around them have noticed the change within them.

This has also happened in my own life.

I desired a particular outcome and yet, I was totally convinced it would take at least six months to implement. I hesitated to take the steps to even get started; I was the one who was now paralysed with my own thoughts, even though I knew I really wanted to see this come to fruition. It was not until my own coach pointed out that it was within my power to change my thoughts and believe that what I wanted could happen more quickly, and more fluidly. As soon as I gave this the power of my new thoughts, the outcome I desired came rushing in.

I have to admit that although as a coach, I had the awareness to do this for myself, my first instinct was to reject it. Sometimes we can be too close to our own challenges and we need to take a step back, or have someone else hold up the mirror for us.

So, I did it.

And as soon as I did, everything relating to this and how I had previously seen it, changed.

Within two weeks of 'changing my mind' or spending time in reprogramming my thoughts, what I had feared would take six months to accomplish manifested itself before my very eyes. This came about, I know, by training my brain about what was possible and changing my beliefs to match my outcomes and areas of possibility.

Imagine what you can accomplish as you let go of your limiting beliefs?

Limiting beliefs tend to lead to dead ends and pits of frustration.

Expanding beliefs can lead you to an open road of possibilities.

# CONTRAST & CHOICE IS EVERYWHERE – SEEK IT OUT

It is amazing how much duality there is in life.

Think of positive and negative reviews at your local restaurant, whatever type of news you are looking for, you will find it.

At any moment in time, you can argue from either side of any issue and win - especially, if you are arguing with yourself - lol.

All you need to do is choose which side to invest in - the one that works for you or against you; the one that shuts you down and keeps you stuck, or the one that releases your wisdom to lead you to a great life.

For many people, it's scary to think that we possess all the power to make that choice.

We also possess the power to defend our beliefs; even those that don't serve us well.

Soon after I started coaching, I suggested to a client that his life could potentially reflect fun and be fun. He looked at me as if I had insulted every last cell in his body and he retorted by telling me that he felt we could not move forward together in a coach and client relationship.

He quite literally fired me on the spot before we had even begun!

Before we parted ways he said, "I am a serious person. Life is serious."

My vision for this man had been so contrary to his entire belief system that his belief system itself went into shock and quite simply could not accept it. His reaction is a great example of how we often cling so tightly to our beliefs, despite their possible negative effect on our life, that we can't see it to be any other way.

And I have also now grown to understand that when people feel that their identity is being attacked they will defend it to no end. Listen carefully, when you hear, "I am" in front of anyone's belief system because it will be the sign for you to know they are accessing a part of their identity that they will usually stand for, fight for and honour.

I tend not to go there with people, unless they have had enough of that side of their identity and are ready and willing to change it.

When you've been married to and carrying around a set of beliefs for a long time, it is as if those beliefs are as familiar to your brain as a riverbed you may navigate year after year on your kayaking adventure holiday.

Your familiarity with that riverbed makes travel for that particular set of beliefs easier and easier. The beliefs flow through by habit, and they flow faster and faster over time, deepening the riverbed the more it continues to flow. Therefore, when it's time to reprogram your brain to work for you it's as if you must portage, which involves picking up your kayak from one navigable river to move onto another.

For you, it means moving your thoughts to a more navigable belief system, one where you will find safe passage to the life you wish to lead.

Certain things in my own life over time have certainly worn a very familiar route in my mind. I can remember two distinct times in my life, the first was the first time in my life I openly admitted to myself when I was eleven, and then expressed this with others at the age of fifteen that I had been sexually abused for twelve years of my life by my step-father, between the ages of three to fifteen. And the other was well into my second diagnosis with cervical cancer, which was followed by the label of being told I only had six months to live - at the time I was twenty-six. My journey with cancer accompanied me for eight years of my life, three times in remission, before I was finally able to set it free.

Depression and not valuing myself for periods of time throughout both of these periods of my life created riverbeds in my life that at the time felt like deep valleys that could not be reached by foot. I felt they were untraversable by me or by anyone for that matter. I had no care in the world as to whether I would actually live or die.

My mind grew accustomed to and knew these riverbeds extremely well. With the slightest trigger, all my energy would flow down that familiar stream of fear and anxiety.

By drawing focus to and understanding my thoughts in these moments, I bit by bit, began to reprogram my thinking and invested the time into understanding the beliefs I had going on. In my own way, I learned how to portage. I learned to pick up my kayak and go to a different river. It has taken me years to make the riverbeds of wiser choices as navigable as those riverbeds of depression and lack of self worth, value and love, but finally I have been able to find a great sense of balance within them now. I have found there are now many riverbeds in which to traverse and they now lead to an abundant place of possibility and choice.

Small events that would normally trigger and release those feelings with the same intensity and destruction as before have become blips on the radar and I now acknowledge them for what they bring rather than fighting them.

Your mental habits may not be as deeply entrenched as mine were.

And you most certainly don't have to have experienced such enduring situations of pain for them to show up in your life.

My point here is to encourage you to listen to your wisdom instead of your limiting thoughts and beliefs. And believe me when I say that reprogramming your thinking and training your brain is the most powerful thing you can ever learn to do for yourself.

Once you decide to choose a more productive thought, taking action is never far behind it, and once you take the action you will see, because of the imprint that it creates for you, that there is always a more navigable riverbed in your mind.

The positive results you obtain through action will cement in your mind that your new expanding beliefs are true.

# ALWAYS LOOK FOR THE EVIDENCE

For a belief to be a defining one, it must be backed up by a tremendous amount of supporting evidence, the evidence that you need in order to make it true. The evidence is your justification for having a belief, for keeping it, and for believing in its power to define and limit you. Once you know how to choose and expand belief, your job is to find new evidence to support the desired belief so you can change the outcome.

Any belief, negative or positive, will dictate any action you will take.

If, like my client Christine, you believe that having lots of money is bad, you might have amassed in your mind a stack of supporting evidence: I will be teased and ridiculed by my friends, I'll be seen as selfish, I'll be corrupted, since money is evil. Christine, who had grown up in a wealthy home, did possess all this mental evidence because these things did happen to her in her youth.

As an adult, however, Christine possessed the ability to seek evidence to support an expanding belief that, as she phrased it, became: "I deserve to make a lot of money". She gathered her own evidence for this as she raised her fees for her consulting services and none of her clients balked.

Christine also saw that her friends never shunned her and she didn't become an evil person. Empowered by her successful business and her expanding belief, she soon joined an Internet Startup, which made her $3million in its first year.

There is a duality in any belief a person holds, a positive side and a negative side.

People make the choice about which side to focus on.

For instance, we all know single people who constantly complain that all women are manipulative or that all men are bad. Since those are their beliefs, these people will be looking for evidence to prove them right. They are likely to miss any evidence to the contrary.

Seeking evidence that supports the flip side (in this example, that there is a kind, intelligent partner out there somewhere) is preferable.

Evidence that supports such an expanding belief will move you along faster and create a positive momentum on its own. If you've ever heard that your beliefs determine the circumstances of your life, this is why.

You may recognise what is wrong in your world view, you may even know what action you need to take to correct your problems, but until your beliefs shift from defining to expanding, you may not even realise that you are the one responsible for the lack of results in your life.

Think of looking through the lens of a camera.

You can see both the foreground and the background, but before you take the picture, you have to choose which to focus the lens on.

The same is true for limiting and expanding beliefs: both are always present, but only the one you focus on can be the more prevalent.

It will always win.

| LIMITING & EXPANDING BELIEFS | |
|---|---|
| *Limiting Beliefs* | *Expanding Beliefs* |
| All men/women are bad | There are good men/women out there |
| Money causes trouble | Money can enable me to achieve what I want |
| I can't trust anyone | I can trust myself to choose whom to trust |
| People my age don't do that | I can do that |
| I have to suffer to be thin | I can be physically fit |
| Everything is so hard | Life can be easy |
| I am not good enough | I am right where I need to be |

# BE SURE TO REALITY CHECK

How do you live large and think bigger, yet still make realisable day-to-day choices?

As you expand your beliefs, you will probably find it necessary to give yourself frequent reality checks in order to make sure you've chosen expanding beliefs that can truly work for you.

The key to determining this is how you feel when you choose a particular belief. If you choose a belief and, instead of it firing you up, it leaves you flat or feeling as if it should have a question mark after it, then you are not yet ready for that expanding belief.

If you choose one that sounds like an affirmation - "I am abundant and powerful", "I am free of pain", or "I am attracting the life of my dreams" - you have probably picked something that you wish were true, but will require some action before it is close enough to your true circumstances to make you feel excited about the possibilities and have a transforming effect.

As you choose an expanding belief, you should look for yourself to be excited and maybe even a bit afraid of its impact - those feelings confirm that you've found one that is true for you.

When you pick the belief, it may feel contrived, so you need to avoid making a quick judgment. Keep in mind that one by-product of having a limiting belief is that they protect us from change, which can be terrifying for some people.

It's normal to return to a limiting belief when we focus on making an expanding belief a reality. Be sure to not run away! Stay put and stay true to what you know lights you up inside.

To make an expanding belief real, choose something that could be true in your life now even if it is not yet a reality. If all that is required to make it a reality is to put focus and effort toward it, you've found the expanding belief that can cause a change in the action you take.

And that is exactly what you are looking for.

Expanding beliefs help you uncover your true desires and form them into beliefs you can create evidence for. An expanding belief is always just real enough to warrant the right evidence. Imagination certainly comes into play, yet the thoughts remain ungrounded in reality. You might want to become a millionaire, but if doing so is really far-fetched, your belief will become a hollow wish for something outside of what is organically available to you at the moment.

An expanding belief is not a wish or a goal. It is a lightning rod held out in front of you to attract evidence that will cause you to change the actions you take. You don't have to give up your desire to become a millionaire, but an expanding belief needs to be rooted close to your present circumstances and resources in order to work easily and well and help you get on the path that may eventually lead you to make such a wish a possibility.

Instead of forcing, "I can be a millionaire", put forward, "I deserve to be financially independent". You will be able to collect evidence and take action much more easily on that one.

Expanding beliefs are yours to hold.

It's your job to name them and choose to put them into effect.

This next coaching exercise is a good first step.

# IT'S TIME TO GRAB YOUR
# 'LYBL' JOURNAL!

## 'LYBL' IN ACTION

Carry your LYBL journal around with you for a day.

Draw a line down the middle of the page so that your page has 2 columns. At the top of the first column on the left hand side write down the heading 'Limiting Beliefs' and on the top of the second column on the right hand side, 'Expanding Beliefs'.

As you go about your daily activities, keep your LYBL journal nearby and record any thoughts that you hold 'true' about yourself, someone else, a situation or life in general.

If it is a thought that stops you, limits you or undermines you, write it down in the 'Limiting Beliefs' column. If it is a belief that supports who you are and what you are trying to accomplish in life, then put it under 'Expanding Beliefs'.

At the end of the 24-hour period, tally how many of each kind of belief or thought you had.

Did you have more limiting beliefs than expanding beliefs?

If you did, that's okay for now, as coming up in this chapter there is a coaching exercise designed to help you turn the ratio around.

Did you have more expanding beliefs than limiting beliefs? Great stuff! Take action and keep collecting evidence to support your mission.

You should now have a clear picture of the quality of your beliefs and the riverbeds that are your brain's natural path. If you're not happy with what you've found, you'll have all the tools you need to change the tides by the end of this chapter.

# 'LYBL' STORY: ENTER DANNI

### BRINGING EXPANDED BELIEFS TO LIFE

Danni had come to attend one of my two day 'Big Business Leadership Club' workshops and sat quietly towards the back of the room. She was tearful, really shy and clearly consumed by insecurities. She really kept to herself until the second morning, when she came to me and described an epiphany she'd had.

After the first day of the program, she had realised that she was in the grips of a limiting belief that she was a worthless person. She had lots of evidence of this, memories of how people had treated her and an overall negative idea of how life had worked out for her. Danni had plenty of ammunition, so much in fact, that she would readily disbelieve or debate anyone who told her otherwise.

Her mission after day one of the program was to select a new expanding belief and then seek concrete evidence of it. Danni's expanding belief was that people were well meaning and she was worth their positive attention. As she caught the train home that night she noticed another woman smile at her for no apparent reason.

Instead of interpreting the woman's gesture as an annoyance, Danni realised that she had found the first evidence that people were kind and that she deserved their kindness. She smiled back.

When Danni arrived on day two, the man sitting beside her offered her a job.

He felt compelled to do so, he said, not out of pity, but because of her willingness and determination to help herself, which he had noticed in her the day before and admired.

To this day, Danni still works for the man and his company and continues to thrive in her work and home life. Danni changed her life by changing one belief.

# IT'S TIME TO GRAB YOUR 'LYBL' JOURNAL!

## 'LYBL' THROUGH WRITING

### Creating Expanding Beliefs

Now it's your turn.

Go back to your list of limiting beliefs and expanding beliefs in your LYBL journal.

Which of your limiting beliefs were the most damaging and limiting?

Transfer those onto a new section of your "LYBL Through Writing" in your LYBL Journal.

If you have several beliefs, do this exercise with each one written separately.

For each limiting belief, write down all the evidence you can think of that belief that is true.

(When Danni did this exercise, her belief was that she was not worth people's kindness. As evidence, she wrote down: "People are not kind to me", "I am not getting through to people I want to be hired by", and "I am not getting along well with some of my closest friends".)

Next, for each limiting belief, write down what the secondary gain is or what is the price you pay to hold onto that belief. For example, Danni's secondary gain was feeling sad, isolated and down on her luck.

Now that you understand the basis of your limiting belief better, let's explore the expanding belief that may be lying dormant and hidden, simply waiting for you to tap into it or activate it.

Write down a result or outcome you would like for your life right now.

For example, Danni chose feeling valued.

Then write down what evidence you would need to see to know that outcome had come to pass. Danni, of course wanted to land a job, but to attain her desired outcome of feeling valued, she also needed to see people treating her with respect.

Finally, ask yourself what belief you think would need to birth for the action necessary to collect/look for the evidence mentioned above. Danni's expanding belief, if you recall from earlier, was that people are well meaning and she was worth their positive attention. This belief allowed her to interact with people from a position of strength.

Look over what you just wrote.

Does it make you feel excited and challenged?

Is it within the bounds of your current life circumstances?

If so, then, yes, this is your new expanding belief.

Now that you've had time to reflect on this coaching exercise, you may want to tweak your expanding belief to be sure that it is one that fits and that you can work with until you've reached the outcome you want.

Remember Mary, whose limiting belief was limiting the possibility of her business's growth?

If we imagine Mary doing this coaching exercise, the outcome she would have wanted would be to increase the income from her business. The evidence required would be more clients, more money, more ease of making things happen.

Mary did the coaching exercise in just this way, and she arrived at the expanding belief that freed her to take action: "I can have a successful business and still have the freedom to enjoy my life".

Once she really believed this, she could create her business the way she wanted it to be.

# 'LYBL' STORY: ENTER RICHARD

## POSSIBILITY IS A CHOICE

Richard, a musician, came to one of my seminars with the limiting belief that the kind of things I did didn't work for him. His girlfriend had bought him a ticket to attend and Richard was clearly an unwilling participant.

So, imagine my surprise when he not only returned for the second day of the seminar but also seemed enthusiastic about the work we were doing. "What happened?" I asked.

"Last night," Richard explained. "I went home and chose an expanding belief that these seminars can work for me. Then, I worked on adopting the belief that people want to hear my music." Overnight, Richard gathered enough evidence of his new beliefs by remembering all the times he'd played his music to great response, and he brought several CD's of his music to the seminar. He sold out before lunch.

His story doesn't end there.

Within a couple of weeks, he was asked to perform at a high-profile event, which truly put his name on the map in the music industry.

# THE KING OF ALL LIMITING BELIEFS

This chapter would most definitely not be complete if I was to skip over the belief that I come up against the most as I coach people.

"I am not good enough" is the king of all limiting beliefs.

It runs rampant in many people's lives and careers.

I know it well, because I too had carried it around with me and held it for a while; you may have it yourself.

I bring it up here because it is so insidious and sneaky that you might not even realise it's running you or even within you.

This belief is so sneaky that it tends to trigger a neediness that keeps the believer running from his true self, chasing his personality's (ego's) needs.

If you happen to hold this limiting belief, you probably have amassed plenty of evidence to support it, and enough pain as a result that looking for evidence to the contrary is a race against the clock and yourself.

You need to know that you ARE good enough, and you often strive to prove this through competitiveness and manipulation of yourself and others. This is no kind of life. The antidote is not to look for evidence that you are good enough at something or another, but rather to find the evidence that you are good as a person.

# 'LYBL' STORY: ENTER DAVID

## BREAKING FREE FROM "I'M NOT GOOD ENOUGH"

David was a newly appointed team leader in a fast growing company. His company appointed me as his coach to help him step into his expanded role, since he had just been promoted within the sales team.

David quickly admitted to me that he felt he was carrying a great weight. He felt insecure in his new position and, in fact, threatened by a peer who seemed to be undermining his every move.

To compensate, David began to exhibit symptoms of what I call the hero syndrome. In an effort to prove how great and worthy he was, David took on endless, unnecessary responsibilities. He began to be a crutch to his team members, taking over their tasks instead of empowering them with responsibility.

He was biting off more than he could chew to feel worthy of their respect.

Without digging to deeply into David's past, it was easy to see that he was trying to fill unmet needs due to a limiting belief he was holding.

The belief was that overall he was not 'good enough'. He had so much evidence that this was true. So together we slowly but surely set out to find evidence that he was, in fact, good.

David had just been promoted - he must be 'good'. He provides for his family and is a much-loved son and brother - he must be 'good'. He knows his business and cares enough to be better at it all the time - he must be 'good'. He is an amazing friend and boyfriend - he must be 'good'!

We had to be able to find some 'good' in there somewhere!

By identifying that David's limiting belief was affecting his world, it allowed him to gain perspective and make some different choices in his life. He could choose to treat that belief as the truth, or not.

David decided to build on the evidence of his 'goodness' that we'd assembled by taking action that reflected his new expanding belief.

He did this by:

- Choosing to go home earlier every day to be the kind of boyfriend he wanted to be
- Developing a better working relationship with his team and the company's Manager
- Looking more empathetically at the man that he felt was his tormenter, and seeing how he was really just as scared as David himself was
- Focusing on how he was 'good', instead of dwelling on how he was not as good as his antagonist

David collected enough evidence of his expanding beliefs that soon he was bitten by his old limiting belief only occasionally. He trained his brain to make the more resourceful choice its automatic choice - and so can you.

# COACHES WRAP UP

**G**etting to where we are meant to be involves acknowledging our current beliefs for all they have provided us up till now and then claiming our new sense of power by reprogramming our thinking to produce new thoughts.

Remember, what got you to here, won't get you to there!

You've got to scratch that record!

To review some things you've learned in this chapter, it's important for you to:

- Notice your well-travelled riverbeds and how deeply grooved they are
- Identify your riverbeds as limiting beliefs
- Change your limiting beliefs to expanding beliefs
- Collect evidence to support your new expanding beliefs
- Keep reprogramming and training your brain until you don't have to any more because you will be taking positive action.

# CHAPTER 3

# DEVELOP A HEALTHY
# PERSPECTIVE

Having a healthy perspective in any challenge or crisis means seeing the situation clearly, in the proper proportion to everything else going on at the same time.

It can be difficult to gauge the appropriate perspective, but generally this involves realising that the situation confronting you is neither the end of the world nor an insignificant blip in your daily life.

Gaining and developing a healthy perspective will help guide you through personal and professional challenges more efficiently, without losing your cool, and without hurting yourself or others.

Still, having perspective on your life can be tough, especially when you are highly analytical about your own life. The tendency is probably to be a bit self-centred.

You are working so hard on understanding yourself that you may forget that you exist in a world filled with many other people.

To gain perspective and move on to have deeper wisdom guiding your life, you need to realise that life in general isn't about you and your immediate world of challenges. You will not arrive at the deeper wisdom that can be yours if you live in the small world of you!

It doesn't mean that you have to have some lofty mission that will touch the masses, but it does mean that for you to experience your best life, you have to get out of the way.

I call this 'getting over yourself'.

So far, we have done a bit of awakening with our mind to be free of its inefficiencies, and in this chapter we will begin to take the focus off our introspective selves.

Now we will begin to leverage what is right about our circumstances, and us and use this awareness to allow our wisdom to come through. With wisdom comes perspective and with perspective comes the freedom to take action that leads to your best life.

When I say, "get over yourself" I mean it as the nicest slap around the head I hope you ever get. Once you realise that what your parents did or did not give you, or what life has given or kept from you, is not a permanent condition, you can set out to change what you feel is wrong. Talk about perspective. You are who and what you are, and you get to renegotiate that with yourself every day.

So get over it and get on with it!

You can start with the ideas in this chapter. We will work together to show you how insignificant you are - and that is a good thing. Don't get me wrong: you are extremely powerful. However, how wisely you use that power will depend greatly on how much self-importance you give yourself.

Getting over yourself is not a matter of assuming a false humility or playing small to not be a threat to those around you. It's about realising that there is so much more at stake in life than your own personal problems. By comparison to the magnitude of crises going on in the world around you, your obstacles can become tame if you want them to be and only if you want them to be!

Why do you think we love to hear about others people's problems so much?

Why are most of us fascinated by disaster?

Because by realising the depth of suffering that can and does exist in this world, we gain perspective.

We gain a brutal understanding of just how fragile life is and how much good there is to embrace.

By absorbing how tiny most of our cares are, we gain the freedom to access them. The information that we need to give us direction and solutions to our problems is accessible once we get over our powerful self-absorption.

# WISDOM IS BLOCKED IN THE FACE OF FEAR

Whenever I ask my clients and program participants what keeps them from doing what they all seem to know they need to do, the answer is always, unequivocally, fear.

Fear - whether in the form of high emotion, anger or dramatic outpourings of panic or just pure drama - is the greatest enemy to your own wisdom.

Wisdom is blocked because of fear's intensity.

Fear is the most insidious and powerfully negative tool the mind has.

Even worse, fear has the capacity to disguise itself as good judgment.

The bad news is that no matter how hard you try to conquer your fears, they will never go away completely.

So your work in this chapter is not to eliminate fear, but to dramatically improve your relationship with it. The first step is to realise that, however much your fear grips you, you have an equal amount of greatness in you.

Our fear is directly proportional to our greatness.

If you are a fearful person, you probably don't have all that you want and do have a tendency to devote more time to your fear than your greatness.

Like hanging out with the 'wrong crowd', it is having a bad influence on you. To improve your relationship with fear you need to get better at knowing when you are experiencing a negative reaction to your circumstances that it's due to fear and not necessarily reality.

Second, it takes knowing what your choices are and third, getting a handle on how to disengage fear's grip on your mind, so that your inner wisdom can flow.

Developing and gaining a healthy perspective is the most significant way to begin to awaken with your fear.

Let's look at some ways to help you gain this perspective on fear so you can move freely towards your best life.

# STOP TAKING THINGS PERSONALLY

When we experience a less than positive exchange with someone or a negative situation in our life, we tend to immerse ourselves in the experience.

We often find it hard to put the conversation in the past or look at what happened with an objective eye. Instead, we take the exchange very personally.

How could we not? It happened to us, right? Yes, but I'm sure you know people - maybe even yourself - who are still suffering over something that happened to them or that someone did to them weeks, months or even years ago.

We often find ourselves unable to move onto a solution because we can't get over what happened. To gain perspective when something bad happens, it is necessary to detach from it, to make the effort to observe the situation objectively.

It's natural to feel disappointed, we must move out of it by separating it from ourselves.

In order to step outside of an event and observe it, you need to increase your self-awareness so that you can catch yourself before you get swept up in and obsessed by the drama of what's going on.

This means, for instance, stopping yourself before you react to a personal attack or an unwanted reaction or circumstance.

For some people, this can be a tall order - but if you can separate, you'll be able to avoid letting the situation get the best of you. You'll be able to form an appropriate response, one that allows you to stretch and become the mature person you want to be in the situation instead of a person who reacts unthinkingly, from primal instinct.

The minute you enter the 'danger zone' with someone and you feel a strong reaction coming on, you need to develop a shield to deflect the bad attitude or harmful words coming at you. You don't want the situation at hand to push your buttons, so the important thing to do is to get this person out of your space gracefully and without contempt.

The secret to being able to develop that shield and not react negatively is to realise that people come from the limit of their own growth and experience. When you accept that their attack on you is really about them and not you, perhaps you can forgive them, accept them and move on. Granted, this may be easier said than done, but when you do it, you maintain the freedom to keep your life moving forward, towards your best life.

Even when you face a tragic circumstance - the loss of a job or a loved one, or the diagnosis of a severe illness - it is not personal.

You were not branded for hard time.

Feel the pain, experience the disappointment, and try to shift yourself to a mind-set of learning all you can from the situation, instead of surrendering to victimhood.

This is the only way forward.

No one wants these things to happen, but even major disappointments hold the potential to turn our heads in the direction of the blueprint for our best life.

# 'LYBL' STORY: RE-ENTER DAVID

### GETTING OVER YOURSELF

Remember David, our young team leader from the last chapter?

I mentioned he had a nemesis at work, someone who just drove him crazy?

David complained to me that this colleague was undermining him, rushing to be the first one to share ideas with management so David would look ineffective in comparison.

David was interpreting this man's actions in a way that made them very personal, as if the co-worker was acting not out of his own self-interest, but out of a desire to hurt David.

So, when David and I looked at this situation together, we discovered that certain buttons of his kept getting pushed.

His own insecurities and feelings of not being good enough (that limiting belief and a very real fear) came up every time.

David finally realised that his 'foe' was not doing anything to him but rather he was doing it to himself. Once he saw this, David was able to 'unhook' by not taking it personally.

He could avoid letting his emotions get the best of him.

David even noticed that there were things he could learn from his 'foe', who possessed a level of confidence that David wanted to emulate and yet was the kind of Manager that David did not want to be.

In fact, instead of feeling in competition with this man, David began to recognise his own unique strengths, many of which were quite different from those of his colleague.

David stopped trying to match his colleague as the 'ideas man' and focused instead on becoming a facilitator for his peers. He began to sit back at meetings instead of looking for the place to jump in with a brilliant new concept.

Instead, he was brilliant at helping people hear one another, and he was a master at encouraging his team to express their ideas clearly.

David became the kind of manager and leader he wanted to be.

David's ability to not take his colleague's actions personally freed him to use his natural talents and be more useful to his company. David got over himself and his brilliance and wisdom were able to shine through.

Not taking things personally is a lesson I have learned vividly throughout the course of my entire life. Doing so has been something I have had to really focus on letting go and replacing with more resourceful strategies.

It seems that this way of life; feeling as if things were always my fault, had followed me around for most of my life, it was all too familiar.

It would leave me feeling trampled.

Most of the time I would walk around feeling annoyed, swearing under my breath. Smiling on the outside, yet feeling torn and ripped on the inside.

Every person who got in my way as I was at my best running this strategy, was to be punished by the intensity of my gaze and the thoughts that followed. Whilst I would often project to the world that it was everyone else's problem, deep down I always felt like things were my fault.

It definitely used to bring up feelings of resentment, the more often I ran it.

Then one day, it most certainly just seem to come from out of the blue, and suddenly I noticed that it was a beautiful sunny day.

It was like the sea had parted and started to let me through. I thought back at all the times where I was carrying around this chip on my shoulder and the feelings of aggravation I was previously living with.

What was different?

What had changed?

There was only one simple answer that my wisdom could acknowledge.

I had.

This day, although I can't remember it's exact and precise date, will be a moment in time I will always remember, I remember where I was, I remember what I was doing and I remember feeling in a happy mood, as if I was emanating a positive energy that glowed at least 3 metres ahead of me.

That glow now lives within me and radiates out to the world every single day, only this time it is real, how I feel on the inside now matches what I am exuding on the outside.

The times where I felt like I was fighting my way through my every day and feeling just as angry towards everyone else around me has now gone. The sea has parted for me and I am more accepting of those around me, and more importantly myself.

I feel no longer to blame for everything,

I no longer takes things personally.

Ease and flow has stepped in and become my everyday way of life.

I am so grateful that this day came and for the work that I did to release my own personal attacks on myself.

Releasing being the blame for everything has been a huge catalyst towards the change I now experience and encounter in my everyday life.

Getting over yourself is something I highly recommend to all of you.

# IT'S TIME TO GRAB YOUR 'LYBL' JOURNAL!

## 'LYBL' THROUGH WRITING

### Release taking things personally

Write down the names of people whom you still hold grudges against or feel less than peaceful about.

(If you don't have any, then good for you, but be sure you're being honest).

Explore what you took personally in each situation.

Did an old friend neglect you?

Did your parents upset you?

Was your neighbor rude to you?

If you were to unhook yourself from the emotion and relive the relationship again what might you do differently?

> What would you say if you ran into this person now?
>
> What could you do to no longer care about what transpired?
>
> Write down specific actions you could take to be sure these scenarios never come back to bite you again.

# TO FIND YOURSELF: MAKE IT ABOUT OTHERS

One of the women attending a recent Australian seminar of mine approached me afterward and told me she was very well known and had been involved in a very public scandal.

I didn't recognise her and she didn't tell me her name or provide any further details. In the aftermath of the scandal, she had been trying to make herself feel better by spending lots of money on shopping and holidays.

She was now seeking some concrete advice about getting her life back on track.

My suggestion was simple: "Get your hands dirty! Go out and hold babies in need or sing to an old person or serve food in a homeless shelter," I said. "You'll find yourself again."

She seemed stunned for a moment but then something seemed to register with her. She thanked me and left.

The advice I gave this woman basically boils down to this: nothing will pull you out of your own stuff faster than realising your stuff isn't so bad.

Intellectually, you know that many other people are worse off than you, but seeing what really is going on in the world first-hand is a wonderful way to put your own life into perspective.

You and your problems are not as important as you think they are.

Nothing will make you realise this more clearly - or make you feel better about yourself - than when there are grateful eyes looking back at you because you improved someone else's condition a little bit.

"That's all well and good," you might say, "but, will it make my problems go away? Will it pay my mortgage? Will it heal my child's life threatening illness?"

Maybe not. But it will give you perspective.

A mountain climber can't get a sense of where she is on the mountain by starting at the ground beneath her feet; she must look up or down to get a sense of where she must go next.

Similarly, through developing a healthy perspective, you may gain clarity to hear your own wisdom directing you to take a certain action or find a resource that can help get you where you want to go.

# IT'S TIME TO GRAB YOUR 'LYBL' JOURNAL!

## 'LYBL' IN ACTION

### Developing a Healthy Perspective

I call this the self-centred challenge.

For an entire week, I want you to strike the word "I" from your vocabulary.

This is the most overused word in the English language, and you'll find it's not easy to avoid.

As you realise how much you use "I", you'll find yourself much more interested in other people.

This exercise may make you feel baffled, humbled or even a little sad.

Such feelings aren't permanent.

They're just the result of your ego's shrinking and feeling very sorry for itself.

Having a healthy ego is not a bad thing, but we could all stand to gain a little perspective in our place in the world.

This perspective invites the ease and satisfaction I've been promising.

# DON'T GO SO FAR THAT YOU LOSE YOURSELF

Although helping others is a very effective tool in helping you gain perspective on your life, it's also important that you not go too far.

If helping someone else results in you neglecting your own life, then it defeats the purpose of gaining a healthy perspective. Being of service to people should not mean sacrificing yourself. When you sacrifice in this way, you end up not getting over yourself but losing yourself.

Giving has nothing to do with loss.

Giving need only be sharing, and when you share, you lose nothing.

However, if you are avoiding your own pain or responsibilities in taking care of others, not only do you not develop or gain a healthy perspective but the help you are giving may actually be less effective than it would be if you were clearly giving to share.

This is because when we overwhelm ourselves with helping other people, we often become resentful, stressed, overburdened and even quite numb.

And when we give to others in a balanced way, we find ourselves instead of losing ourselves in the process.

## CREATE SPACE

Besides doing for others and not taking things personally, a healthy perspective can come from simply getting some distance from a situation.

By creating space.

This can be done literally: if you are having trouble at work, get up and go outside for a walk to take yourself out of the environment that's causing you so much stress.

Even if you are in the middle of something, break your thinking pattern by clearing your head with a walk and you'll be so much more productive when you get back.

Creating space and gaining distance can also be metaphorical.

Sometimes we need mental space more than physical space.

If you are having trouble with a relationship, try moving your mind away from it by engaging your creativity.

Draw a picture about how you feel, do some work on a workshop or start a project, read a short story or even a children's book. All these activities take you somewhere else mentally and are sometimes enough to gain the perspective you need to come back to the relationship and deal with the issues more objectively.

If literal and metaphorical distance don't release the grip your mind has on you, I'm afraid you'll have no other choice then to give in and laugh.

# LAUGHTER REALLY IS THE BEST MEDICINE

"Oh, come on, lighten up".

Don't you just love hearing that when you feel like you have a justifiable reason for not being happy?

Yet by suggesting that perhaps you need to chill out or adjust your attitude, these people may not realise just how very astute and wise they are being in their request.

Wisdom alone cannot get through when your thoughts are dense or heavy.

Laughter lightens the mind's load and relieves the tension that keeps your heavy thoughts circling around and around.

Laughter can free your thoughts from their tendency to go down a negative riverbed. Laughter distracts you from what's bothering you, giving you a sense of detachment that allows your intuition to kick in.

As a result, it enables your mind to make room for unusual solutions to problems as well as for wisdom to come through. It allows you to get in touch with the part of you that is wiser and might be more rational than your emotional self.

Laughter dulls the edge of the knife your inner critic wields.

Since it can do all these things, is it any wonder that we are grateful for comic relief during a serious movie or play or even an intense business meeting?

## 'LYBL' STORY: ENTER STEPHEN

Stephen is a wonderful example of someone who just needed to laugh. He sat in the front row at one of my seminars and seemed riveted by what I had to say.

When I asked for a volunteer to come up on stage, he stood up and asked for my help.

He wanted to have more fun in his life, he declared.

With all due respect, Stephen was far from being completely all doom and gloom, but he looked as if he hadn't cracked a smile in many years.

Intuitively, I knew that if he was to have any chance at having more fun, he needed to have a reference point for it immediately.

So I began to laugh and asked him to join me. It wasn't easy for him, so I asked the audience to join us. Soon, the whole place was in tears as we laughed until our sides ached.

Finally, I saw a real laugh emerge from Stephen.

When it did, his skin practically changed colour. He was benefiting from increased oxygen and his face changed to pink from ashen. He experienced fun, even if only for a moment.

He turned to leave the stage with a demure "thank you", and then suddenly turned back, gave me a huge hug, and shouted as if it surprised himself: "I can have fun!".

# IT'S TIME TO GRAB YOUR 'LYBL' JOURNAL!

## 'LYBL' IN ACTION

### Lighten Up & Laugh

Find a humour mentor, someone whose sense of humour you just love.

Study this person, what he or she finds funny, where their humorous outlook on life comes from.

If you are already a fun lover, stretch yourself even further.

Get a DVD or download some YouTube clips of a professional comedian who appeals to you.

Watch and listen for how he or she looks at life to find its humour.

If you really want to stretch, how about enrolling in a stand-up comedy class?

Think of this as training for your mind.

Just as there are times when helping others crosses the line, we need to be careful with laughter as a way of gaining perspective.

That's because it can sometimes serve to hide our true feelings.

And it's common for people to deflect intimate, deep emotions with humour to avoid feeling vulnerable.

I once attended a wedding where the bride cracked jokes and played up to the guests during the ceremony because she was terribly uncomfortable with the profound sanctity of the moment.

Humour is also used as a way of expressing an opinion without being genuine.

I'm sure you can think of many times in your life when someone cracked a joke at your expense, only to take it back, upon seeing your reaction, with an indignant "Just kidding".

In fact, the person being kidded was not you but the joker, who convinced himself that you would not notice or feel the true intention behind his humour.

When humour is used to avoid telling the truth, it loses its ability to clear your brain and allow your inner wisdom to emerge.

When humour is truthful, it can be just as powerful in its impact as a profound philosophical insight.

Just as a profound insight can illuminate a new possibility, so can humour provide a way to look at something in a whole new way.

# 'LYBL' STORY: ENTER JAMES

## USING JOKES AS A MASK

James was a well-liked businessman who was known in his community for his sense of humour. I was engaged to coach some of his key people and in the process; I became his coach as well.

Through talking to him first hand and hearing about his behaviour from his team colleagues, I quickly learned that he tended to use humour as a weapon instead of addressing people's problems in a more honest way.

He'd say, "If you'd gone to a good school, you'd have been able to figure this out," or, "Keep dressing like that and we'll be attracting every pervert in the country."

Not very nice – nor very effective.

When I pointed out to James that he seemed unable to communicate what he really felt in an appropriate way, he reacted defensively.

After a few weeks, however, he finally admitted that he knew he was sometimes hard on people and thought that using humour was a way to soften his blows. He saw this was a cop-out, allowing him to not take responsibility for what he was saying - because, after all, it was just a joke.

Together, James and I worked on ways in which he could communicate more honestly. Every time he was about to make a wisecrack, he made an effort to stop himself and ask first, "What am I not communicating here?"

He could then address the real issue.

For example, instead of the wisecracks he would use above, he could say things like: "We're all under a lot of pressure, but let's do our best to find a solution to this problem," or "I'm concerned that your attire doesn't reflect the kind of respect for your position that will encourage others to respect your work."

Over the course of a few months, James began to see a dramatic increase in sales among his associates. They freely admitted feeling more energised and motivated about their work once James' acerbic humour stopped and honest feedback and conversations stepped in.

The bottom line is that humour and laughter can transform us and those around us in a positive way - as long as they are not being used to hurt, or to gain or wield power.

# CHOOSE LOVE

Another tool that we can draw upon to shift our perspective is love.

We've all heard the merits of loving ourselves, loving others and loving the planet, right?

But not all of us have been able to use all that love to positively affect the daily transactions of our lives.

The pace of our lives and the intensity of our emotions or personality often prevent us from acting with love as a code.

It may be hard to be kind to others, or ourselves or to face a critical situation with the perspective love can provide.

In order to think of love as a fundamental code, one by which we can live, it may help to compare it with another code, one by which many of us are already guiding our lives: power.

In the time we live in, power is still defined very much by external references, such as money, status, position or the ability to influence others.

We are powerful if we have these things and powerless if we don't.

They can be taken away.

Love cannot be taken away.

You can always choose to love someone, something or a situation, whether you feel those things merit love or not.

That is true power.

Love, as a choice, is power.

Instead of choosing to hate, fight, undermine or manipulate, you could choose to love, and that choice might help you find a more positive solution to any problem.

For example, if someone betrayed my friendship, I could decide to banish that person from my life and forever speak of how he did me wrong. On the other hand, I could gain a quick exit to the pain by choosing love to find perspective.

I don't have to agree with what the person did, nor do I have to forgive them. I just have to choose to love them and myself and elevate myself to the place where I can see they did me a favour.

Now I know he was not as true a friend as I thought, and I can go on in my life with a lesson learned. A much more powerful choice, I think, than holding onto bitterness, even though many would feel I was justified to do so.

When it comes to love, we often don't honour ourselves enough and therefore have little or no wisdom-producing perspective.

Loving yourself or someone else does not mean abandoning self by overindulging in the feeling or its intoxicating effects.

It doesn't mean sacrificing yourself to love someone or even merely to have another person like you.

It means harnessing your emotion and awareness to create the most good in your life.

That means that if a relationship is destructive, you should get out.

It's not an invitation to love harder.

There is no power in loving harder - only in loving better.

# 'LYBL' STORY: ENTER JANE

## GAINING PERSPECTIVE BY CHANGING WHAT LOVE MEANS TO YOU

Jane was a smart woman in her early thirties who came to me to do some career and life planning. She was engaged to an older man who had children from a previous marriage and did not want any more. Jane worked for a large bank but longed to own her own business someday. We had come up with a plan to improve her satisfaction with her current job, which included asking for a pay rise and revamping her responsibilities.

Naturally, as we discussed her career, Jane's impending wedding kept coming into the conversation.

I had a strong sense that this marriage was a mistake, yet I withheld my judgment.

As we explored her job, her desired new business and her upcoming marriage, it was clear to me that Jane's definition of love was erring on the side of self-sacrifice.

She was struggling with the realisation that by marrying this man she was giving up the chance to have children of her own. It wasn't appropriate for me to tell Jane what to do, yet I did tell her how I felt: "What I want for you, Jane, is a relationship where you don't have to bend over backwards in order to fit in."

She seemed hardly to acknowledge my comment, however two weeks later she reported that she had ended her engagement. She was quitting her job and taking a long trip abroad in order to explore herself and her life.

Until then, Jane's meaning of love was to do what everyone else wanted her to, and to love harder meant giving up more of herself to make it work.

When she learned to love differently and therefore learned to love herself, her perspective changed. She saw that choosing to love herself meant that she had to reclaim the pieces of herself she had compromised.

Once she made the change, the direction she needed to take was clearer and the action she took immediate.

Wisdom had replaced anxiety and confusion.

She had gained the perspective that gave her clarity to do the right thing for herself.

# WHERE YOUR FIND YOUR PERSONAL POWER, YOU WILL FIND LOVE

**M**ost people think that loving ourselves means accepting ourselves for who we are, shortcomings and all, and being nice to ourselves with gifts and nurturing gestures.

That's part of it.

But the greatest love of self is keeping an eye on where we distribute our power.

Earlier I said that choosing to love, even in adverse situations, was a way to gain perspective, and define true power.

Now I take that one step further to say that watching where you distribute that power reflects on how well you love yourself.

Do you choose to love out of fear in order to protect yourself from a consequence, or do you love out of fear in order to protect yourself and other people?

When you choose to love from fear, you are not loving yourself, you are doing what you think you have to in order to get what you want.

When you respect yourself and therefore love yourself, you will get what you want and with more ease and satisfaction.

You will not be compromising yourself.

As a coach, I spend a lot of time assisting people reclaim their own sense of personal power.

They do this not by stealing it from a friend or a boss, but by reclaiming pieces of themselves they have given away over time, when they really did not want to, whether in a relationship, a business deal, a meeting, or another detail of their life.

The place to begin amassing power is within yourself.

Look at where you are giving it away.

Look for the places where it is leaking out of you like air from a punctured tyre.

It is usually not hard to locate: is it where you are abandoning yourself, where action must now be taken?

Getting that power back and keeping it should be what it is to love yourself.

# 'LYBL' STORY: ENTER KIM

## CONNECTING BACK TO YOUR SOURCE OF POWER

Kim, a housewife, came to me because she wanted to become more assertive in communicating with her partner and friends.

In listening to her speak, it was soon clear to me that she needed to recognise how often she gave away power by unnecessarily apologising for herself.

On the phone, she would start a conversation by saying, "I'm sorry, is Michele there?"

She was sending signals that she had weak boundaries and could be counted on to overextend herself to please others.

Once I pointed it out to her, Kim watched herself very closely. She listened for how often she apologised for herself. In shops, she would ask an assistant, "If you have a moment, could you possibly stop to help me with this purchase?" At the bank she would say to the teller, "I don't mean to bother you, but when could you be free to talk with me?" And when a friend reached for a serviette in her kitchen, she'd rush to help and say, "Oh, I'm sorry, I should have done that for you."

She had never been conscious of how often she betrayed herself with her words.

Discovering how often she put the needs of others first in her speech changed Kim's world. She removed 'apology language' from her vocabulary. She soon began to stand up straighter, speak louder and articulate what she wanted more quickly.

In just a few months, the people in Kim's life were acknowledging how she had changed. Her newfound self-confidence allowed her to connect back to her own source of personal power and reclaim it in her relationship by no longer being afraid of conflict and by addressing matters head-on with her partner.

It also allowed her to negotiate part ownership of a clothing shop to which she had previously given a great deal of time without asking for anything in return.

Overall, she felt the quality of almost all of her relationships was higher and more pleasurable.

She no longer felt like everyone's doormat, with no tools to help herself.

Connecting back to her source of personal power required first that she improve her relationship with herself, which in turn transformed her relationships with others.

Everything must always begin and end with us.

# IT'S TIME TO GRAB YOUR 'LYBL' JOURNAL!

## 'LYBL' IN ACTION

### Connect back to your source of Personal Power

**I**t's time for action!

I challenge you in the next week to increase the power you have by taking it back from where it does not belong.

Examine the recent past, looking for situations in which you have compromised yourself.

Record in your LYBL Journal what these situations were, and be specific about what happened and who was involved. If you were disappointed by a friend who did not keep a promise, for example, and you were afraid to ask about it, write:

"Mark said he would visit this weekend and then did not turn up or phone to say he wasn't coming. I didn't call him about it, although it's the second time he's done something like this."

In every situation you've written about, think about what you can do to reverse the loss of power.

Your perspective will be changed as you see your power increase and as you realise that the key to moving your life forward in a positive way has roots in this kind of self love.

# A LOT CAN BE SAID ABOUT GRATITUDE

One more way of gaining and developing a healthy perspective on your life is though expressing gratitude.

Showing that you are grateful for what you have multiplies your ability to attract what you think you lack.

If you choose to validate what you lack by harping on about it, you are draining yourself of the energy you need to focus on what you have that can be leveraged to your great benefit.

As your coach, I am always looking for what's right about you to help you build your future.

Recognising how much you already have and being grateful for it is key to accomplishing the future.

Taking stock of what's working lessens the leaden effect of focusing on what is missing.

It turns up the volume on possibility.

Finding out what you're grateful for allows you to move forward more quickly.

I can't tell you how many people have approached me, bitter about what their jobs or life circumstances, only to hear me ask "What can you be grateful for?"

They look at my quizzically, but I continue:

"What have you learned from your unsatisfying experience?

Did you learn a new skill?

Have you discovered what tasks or circumstances no longer suit you? Great!

Now what do you have to be grateful for?

Now what do you have to do?"

# 'LYBL' STORY: ENTER JOHN

## GRATITUDE AS YOUR SAVIOUR

Things had not been going John's way. He hated where he lived, he resented his wife's inability to snap out of a bad mood, and he was not satisfied with his career.

There wasn't a whole lot in his life that he felt grateful for.

Although John was struggling to overcome all these circumstances, nothing he did seemed to break him free of his frustrations and dissatisfaction.

It was time for John to get over himself and gain a healthy perspective on his life.

John took stock of his material possessions, his work experience and his marriage.

In all three categories, he had much to boast of.

John saw that his current work had given him the experience he needed to pursue a dream position he'd recently heard about in Sydney.

He saw that he had much to appreciate about his wife and that he had learned a lot about himself by being in his relationship with her.

While this helped bring them closer together, it also ultimately led them to the decision that separating would be the best step for both of them.

As John was searching for something to be grateful for about the small town where he lived, he realised that at the least it had convinced him that he belonged in a cosmopolitan city.

Up to this point, John had been feeling victimised; gratitude had been the last thing on his mind.

Once he changed his focus from the negative in his life to the positive, he gained a new perspective and was able to see clearly what he needed to do next.

John had been in pain, but instead of taking his anger, frustration and disappointment out on others, or inflicting punishment on himself, he turned inwards and was able to set himself free by multiplying what was good about his life.

John ended up moving to Sydney, where he accepted his dream job.

His life opened up, and he felt more alive than he had in years.

# IT'S TIME TO GRAB YOUR 'LYBL' JOURNAL!

## 'LYBL' THROUGH WRITING

### What are you Grateful for?

Taking stock of what you can be grateful for on a daily basis becomes an important way to make this way of developing and gaining a healthy perspective a habit.

Try it now by writing down ten things you can be grateful for today.

These could be your health, your family, the roof over your head, your job, your money, your new car, your neighbor, your friends and so on.

It could also be more circumstance oriented – such as a particularly good conversation with a co-worker, or a chance meeting with a long-lost friend, or the fact that a woman in the supermarket queue gave you her place so you could check out sooner.

Now go back to the complaints about your life that you listed in Chapter 1.

Look at them with your new set of eyes and try to find something to be grateful for about the items that are problems now.

What have you learned from having these problems – how are they stretching you and forcing you to grow?

As annoying as they may be, examining them through the lens of gratitude may uncover the hidden positives about them.

As a third part to this writing, write down how your perspective has shifted because of this activity.

What might you do differently?

Is there any action you would like to take now because of it?

Write down the changes you will make.

# COACHES WRAP UP

Gaining and developing a healthy perspective is the third and final strategy of 'Your Awakening' stage.

A healthy perspective on your life will assist in putting you on track to where you are meant to be.

Working to maintain the right perspective is a lifelong investment, and you've learned a variety of techniques that will enable you to do that.

Even when things are going well for you, remember to:

- Avoid taking things personally
- Let go of old grudges
- Assist other people
- Say 'I' less
- Look for humour
- Create space
- Choose to love
- Reclaim your power by loving yourself
- Focus on what you have to be grateful for instead of what you don't have

# PART TWO

# YOUR ACTIONS

*"Your part is to awaken your desire to accomplish your worthy objectives. Then whip your will into action until it follows the way of wisdom that is shown to you"*

— *Paramahansa Yogananda*

**M**astering your physical world by 'doing' - that is, by putting your wisdom into action - is the key to unlocking the magic of your best life.

In this section we will address two aspects of your physical world: your physical body and the life circumstances around you.

First, I'll show you how to observe yourself and your surroundings with more care and then we'll work on searching your innate wisdom for the actions that can truly make a difference in finding what you want.

This will allow you to get off the 'trying to have it all' treadmill that most of us live on.

This part of the book will show you what keeps you in overdrive and how to get out.

Taking action is the key.

Recognising the right action to take is mastery.

I find that many people chase success, hoping it will somehow fill the void they have not been able to fill in their lives. They don't realise that if they were to stop and find ways to become responsible for their present circumstances, they could begin to master their lives.

The future they crave will then have a safe landing strip.

Chasing the future keeps what you want at bay.

Accepting responsibility for the present invites your extraordinary future to come and find you.

The physical world is your testing ground.

It tests your spirit, your survival skills, your intelligence, and everything in between.

Most of us assume that the test is to 'make it' - to succeed, to make our parents proud, to make something of ourselves.

If only we knew that acing the test requires simply that we do everything in our power to make our life work.

This does not necessarily mean you will be granted an idyllic life.

Making your life work does not guarantee you'll have everything you want, but it will mean that the struggle has been reduced and fulfilment has returned.

It requires becoming attuned to what must stay and what must go in your life at any given moment and being honest about what you really want instead of settling only for what you think you can have or should have.

As a result, you will feel like you are creating your life by your own choices, not from a list of obligations and expectations you feel trapped by.

In order to make this happen, we will examine your life closely to determine where you should spend your time and energy to get the most from your life.

You will learn to discern the clues your body can give you about living your best life.

After that, you'll make your very own personal manifesto to underscore with action all the emotional awakening you did in Part One.

From there, you'll discover that you come equipped with a 'lucrative purpose' - something you are meant to be doing in life that will satisfy you physically, spiritually and financially.

Finally, you will learn how to magnetise yourself - attracting positive outcomes to yourself and repelling negative ones by allowing your innate wisdom to guide your physical action.

One might say this is the beginning of the fun part, others say it is the beginning of an entirely new life, their best life.

# CHAPTER 4

# LISTEN TO YOUR FEELINGS & ALLOW THEM TO GUIDE YOU

Up until now, we have focused on what you are thinking rather than on what you are doing in your life.

After all, your thoughts and words determine the actions you'll be willing to take.

You can't just think yourself to that point.

Here we will start to integrate your mind with your body.

We are going to raise awareness of your body to determine the actual actions that will get you to live your best life.

Beyond thinking, to experience wisdom you have to feel and know what you are feeling.

We can all recognise feelings like anger, frustration, sadness, elation and love - extreme emotions are easy to identity.

Yet, the clues to our best lives do not lie in the extremes, but rather in our more subtle feelings, such as sensing the difference between passion and adrenaline or between inspiration and ego.

To recognise subtle feelings, we need to be sensitively attuned.

We must be in a state of calm to fully feel them.

Too often we are simply too busy, exhausted, overwhelmed, anxious or revved up to find that necessary calm.

We become desensitised to the subtleties of feeling by adrenaline, busyness, distractions, dramas and the self-centredness of chasing what we want. We become numb to our emotions because we get into the habit of avoiding feelings that make us uncomfortable or that demand we take time to deal with them.

Doing as much as we do in our busy worlds, on a daily basis, causes most of us to rev our bodies into overdrive, running on adrenaline in order to have the energy to meet our demands.

Running on adrenaline stresses our bodies.

It's something we're equipped to do for only short periods of time.

But we often are in overdrive for longer periods, which eventually wears down our systems.

Too much stress can result in physical or emotional exhaustion, mood swings, insomnia, even illness and disease.

Our work in this chapter is to get you off the 'busy' treadmill of your life by getting you in touch with what you really feel and want on a visceral level.

I will guide you to learn to admit your feelings, to feed them deeply and to be so sensitive to them that you are never so busy in your daily life to ignore them.

You will begin to feel your way to the awareness required to be in partnership with your body and your life, rather than being run by them.

Once you recognise your feelings, you will begin to trust them to guide you to actions that can affect your life positively and immediately.

## LISTEN TO THE SUBTLETIES IN YOUR FEELINGS

Your body holds the clues to the blueprint of your best life.

Let's take a look at what may be in the way of you feeling the subtleties of your own wisdom as expressed in your own body.

## IT'S TIME TO GRAB YOUR 'LYBL' JOURNAL!

Place a tick on the line next to each statement below that you would say is true about you.

| 'LYBL' IN ACTION | |
|---|---|
| **Are Your Hearing Your Feelings?** | |
| I work more than 70% of my day | |
| I exercise fewer than 3 times a week | |
| I live on the edge financially | |
| I have great conflict in some of my relationships | |
| I drink more than one caffeinated beverage per day | |
| I'd like more quality time with my family | |

| | |
|---|---|
| I need more space in my home | |
| Emotional issues often get in my way | |
| I have outstanding bills and paperwork | |
| People always depend on me | |
| I abuse alcohol and / or drugs | |
| I have strained personal relationships | |
| My work environment impedes productivity | |
| I wish for a more satisfying life | |
| I engage in fun activity fewer than twice a week | |
| I have more than my share of problems | |
| I overpromise my time and what I can accomplish | |
| I am self conscious about my appearance | |

Give yourself 1 point for each tick. Tally your score and analyse the results and what they mean to you with the guidelines below.

**1-2:** Congratulations! You are probably in touch with most of what challenges you, and you can see where the blemishes are. Now is the time to take action on them so you are free to follow your own wisdom.

**3-6:** You've started to enter the 'unconscious zone' where you are becoming resigned to the circumstances in your life. It's not an ideal state for hearing your own wisdom and being connected to what you feel.

**7-10:** Life must feel terribly overwhelming to you. You're not in a place where wisdom can be heard. Radical action will be required.

**11 or more:** You are completely in reactive mode, barely keeping your head above water. It would be almost impossible to hear yourself think, much less decipher how you feel and what you really want.

The things mentioned in the above quiz are distractions. They take up a lot of time and energy and yet they're exactly what keep you from feeling that you have what you want. They point you away from yourself, not towards yourself.

What you truly desire may be getting sacrificed to the demands of your daily life.

Things don't have to be this way.

Our work in 'Your Actions' will help you expand your scope out of what is possible, so your life can revolve around what matters to you most.

In order to connect with your body and its emotions to find your wisdom's clues, let's first evaluate how far your daily activities have taken you away from what you say truly matters to you.

## THE GAP IS WHERE IT IS AT: THIS IS YOUR POTENTIAL ZONE

Write down the things you most want for your life, in order of importance.

This could be health, well-being, family, romantic relationships, friends, leisure, hobbies, career, spiritual life, adventure, education, personal growth etc.

It's been shown that we can do only three to five things at a time if we are to do them well.

Your next step is to choose five items from your list and put them in order of priority.

The item you would want if you could be granted only one thing in life should be written down first. Item 2 is what would be important if you could have just one more thing. Continue until your list has a maximum of five items.

Here's an example of what one list might look like at this point:
1. Health
2. Friends and Family
3. Career
4. Personal Growth
5. Fun and Recreation

To the right of each item jot down the order in which those things appear in your life now.

For example, if I say health is the number one priority in my life, but I haven't exercised regularly in six months, it might really merit a score of five. And if I don't do anything to improve or maintain my health at all in my real life, then I'll put a zero in that column.

You may have a few zeros, but don't worry - you're not alone.

Every audience I have ever shared this with has a predominance of zeros in the line up.

The finished version of the list might be something like.
1. Health 5
2. Friends and Family 2
3. Career 1
4. Personal Growth 0
5. Fun and Recreation 0

Our hypothetical coachee says his health is important, but he does almost nothing about it.

He wants to have friends and feel connected to the community, but he does even less in those areas.

If you see a lot of zeroes on your list, my strategy has succeeded.

In having you take the quiz, I want to wake you up to the fact you are not spending time doing what you say is important to you.

You are probably spending your time trying to accomplish all you think has to come before you are allowed to reward yourself by attending to your own desires.

No, no, no! Living this way desensitises you to what you really want.

This, in turn, is leading you further and further away from your goal - the life you want to be living.

# GET BACK IN TOUCH WITH YOUR FEELINGS

By now you've assessed what kinds of things may keep you living a 'treadmill existence' and you've got a clearer picture of what keeps you from having the time for the things that matter to you most.

In my experience as a coach, when people are pulled in several directions this way, it is hard to create a significant forward motion, goal attainment, and satisfaction in life.

The antidote is to get back in touch with what you truly want and get back to feeling again.

When you make contact with your feelings, you can sense when you have betrayed yourself by taking on yet another obligation that distances you from your goals and priorities.

Obviously, obligations like turning up for work in the morning can't be avoided, but when you get back in touch with what you feel, you may have to admit that even your job could warrant some changing.

Obligations become 'shoulds' in your life - the things you think you must do and over which you think you have no power.

It is the 'shoulds' that keep you away from what is important to you.

Here's what you do:

- Memorise your list of priorities
- Use the memorised list as a measuring stick against every demand on your time
- Arrive at the point where you can sense your true priorities in your cells

Eventually, you will not let anything come between you and what truly matters.

You can change the list in the preceding exercise over time, but always keep it at five items. It's critical to feel the difference between a true desire and everything else that vies for your attention.

It is critical that you trust this feeling.

# LISTEN TO WHAT YOU WANT

So many times we ignore what we want (what we feel) in the name of what we think we can or should have.

We are so fast to doubt or complicate what we truly desire with excuses, preconceived notions of what's possible and limiting beliefs, before we have even tried to make our desire come to fruition.

The worst part is we don't even know we are doing it.

We hear the wisdom of the desire, but immediately dismiss it in favour of what we think we can have.

# 'LYBL' STORY: ENTER LUCAS

During one of my 'Live Your Best Life' workshop webinars, Lucas, a salesman, asked me to coach him on how we could increase his sales figures. When I asked him how many sales he wanted and how he could go about getting them, he never seemed emotionally connected to this goal.

So I asked him what he really wanted.

He repeated an amount in dollars and how many sales that would require. But his voice was again flat and there was no excitement behind it.

"No," I said "If you were really honest, and I could wave my magic coaching wand and you could have it right now, what would you want?"

Lucas thought for a minute, then his voice lit up. "My own business".

The minute he said this, Lucas realised he had been settling for what he thought he could have instead of what he truly wanted.

He really wanted his own business, but he was settling for more sales instead.

The next time I heard from him, just a few weeks later, Lucas had advanced himself and was pursuing his dream of becoming an entrepreneur.

Most of us do what Lucas was doing.

We ignore what we truly want, thinking we can't possibly have it, and then proceed to get frustrated with the lack of results we see or the lack of motivation we experience as we try to accomplish the goal we set in consolation.

Life gives us what we expect it to give us.

In other words, we get what we expect.

In fact, if truth be known, we actually create it to be that way.

Breaking through the bigger possibilities isn't about positive thinking, nor is it reserved for the privileged.

Breakthroughs occur when you respect the wisdom you are wired for.

Getting in touch with what you truly want accomplishes that.

When the wisdom that is yours speaks to you, take the message seriously and stop pre-empting it.

# THE SMALL THINGS ARE ALWAYS THE BIG THINGS

So how do you get in touch with what you're feeling?

How do you distinguish between the subtle desires that lead you towards accomplishing a goal easily and the sometimes overwhelmingly rational instructions your brain sends that lead to much more difficulty and stress in your life?

It takes practice.

You can learn to feel the subtle distinctions between feelings. Then you will increase the speed at which you process information and attract positive outcomes.

How you get there, however, is usually by trial and error. By deliberately and consistently paying attention to when your emotions tell you, "I want this" vs. your thoughts saying, "I should do this".

There are dozens of subtleties.

Let's look at a few of them.

# IT'S TIME TO GRAB YOUR 'LYBL' JOURNAL!

## 'LYBL' IN ACTION

### Feeling Subtleties

This activity will start you on your way to becoming more sensitive to the difference between 'want' and 'should' – the first subtlety we will explore.

### The ........................ Day

This activity is called 'The..........Day' because you fill your name in the blank and the first step is to find a day that you can keep blank, or completely open.

Take a whole day and leave it free, with no plans or obligations at all.

On this day, no-one is to need you or demand anything of you (not even your dog), nor can you demand anything of yourself.

Setting aside an entire day to do this may seem like a huge request. I know it is if you have kids. If doing this is impossible for you, you can experience a similar effect by giving yourself just a few hours of completely blank time.

Starting right at the beginning of the period you've set aside, I want you to constantly ask yourself, "What do I want?"

If the answer is that you want pancakes for breakfast, have them. If you want to dance around the house to loud music, terrific. If you want to play golf or curl up with a good book, do it.

Whatever it is, as long as it won't hurt you or someone else, indulge! Remember, we are all about ecology!

As you physically give yourself to whatever you've told yourself you wanted, I'd like you to notice what you feel (My clients often report feeling the joyful kind of wanting in their heart, their solar plexus area, or their stomach, or a tingling in their fingers or all over their body).

There is no right answer, so just get to know your sensations for yourself.

You probably know what 'should' feels like.

You're anxious, bothered, perhaps confused?

Some people feel it in their head, or in their solar plexus, or in the chest and neck. It doesn't matter where it registers, as long as you are now aware of the different physical sensations of 'should' and 'want'.

Use your 'LYBL' Journal to record your observations on your..............day

As you increase your awareness through this exercise, you won't have to think so hard about it, you'll just make quicker decisions because you are sensitive to how 'want' and 'should' feel.

# GUILT – TWO SIDES OF THE COIN

As you learn to distinguish between 'want' and 'should', you will probably experience one feeling that you'll have no trouble identifying. When you begin to feel what you really want and recognise how much you have denied your wants in the past, guilt usually starts to show its all-too familiar face.

You'll need to distinguish 'good' guilt from 'bad' guilt as you let your own wisdom direct the path of your work and life.

Here, we will take a closer look at the hidden messages of guilt and how to interpret them.

'Good' guilt is the kind that taps you on the shoulder and says, "Hey, before you do that, take a look inside to see if you will have any regrets about this decision."

Listening to your feelings of 'good' guilt before you take an action will help you figure out whether you might:

- Regret expanding your career to another city (or not taking it)
- Regret confirming a friend on an issue (or not doing so)
- Regret being at work instead of staying home with your kids while they are growing up
- Regret taking five years out of your career to raise kids

No matter how it plays out, 'good' guilt is trying to tell you something and can help you formulate a decision that will work for you.

'Bad' guilt, on the other hand, is unnecessary angst delivered by an outside messenger that echoes your loudest fears. It says you are a lousy manager, a bad friend, a terrible sibling because it shamelessly compares you to an unachievable ideal.

When you notice feelings of guilt, ask yourself whether they are based on what other people will think if you don't do 'x' or if you do 'y'.

If so, that is not wisdom speaking to you.

It's your ego sneaking in another 'should'.

Thank it for its opinion and for showing up and then set it free.

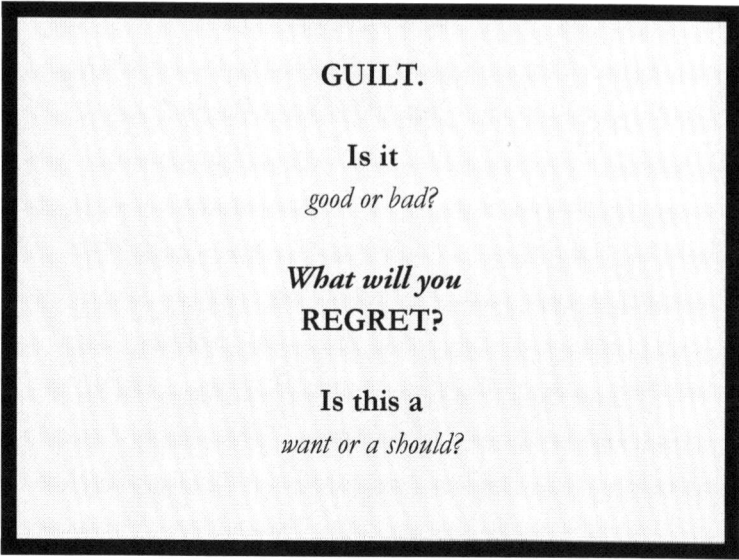

# 'LYBL' STORY: ENTER PAUL

### 'BAD' GUILT WILL HOLD YOU BACK

Paul was a top business leader who came to me when he was about to let go one of his senior team leaders.

He was feeling a tremendous guilt about this move, not only arguing with other team members over it, he was also experiencing physical symptoms: he couldn't sleep, he had painful stomach aches and he often caught himself clenching his jaw.

He knew that letting this person go was essential to the success of his business, but personally he felt guilty because he felt he could have done more to help this person succeed.

I explained the difference between 'good' guilt and 'bad' guilt to him, and asked him which he as experiencing.

Paul saw that his rumblings were a product of 'bad' guilt.

Using regret as a barometer, there wasn't anything compelling enough to keep him from taking action. He could say that he regretted not having tried harder, but in taking a second look that wasn't really true.

His anxiety and confusion were due to having set up a standard for himself against which he was inaccurately measuring his success as a manager.

He had created an unspoken rule that he had to have the grit and leadership qualities to make every situation work or he wasn't 'good' or capable.

I asked Paul to think about the action that was needed in this situation from a different angle. Instead of asking himself, "What should I do?" (let this person go), the new question Paul posed was, "What do I need to do to make my organisation work?" Here the answer was: "Let go of a team leader who is keeping us from being successful."

When Paul thought in terms of what he wanted - a functional, smoothly running business - his physical symptoms of stress and anxiety disappeared.  .

# 'LYBL' STORY: ENTER WENDY

## 'GOOD' GUILT CAN SET YOU FREE

$P$aul has been experiencing 'bad' guilt, which can be incapacitating.

'Good' guilt, on the other hand, has unique and positive qualities.

Wendy, another client, had accepted a once-in-a-lifetime career opportunity in another city, but she could not seem to shake feelings of guilt about moving her family to a new home and asking her husband to uproot his career.

When I asked Wendy to think about 'good' guilt versus 'bad' guilt, she saw that her true feelings had more to do with a sense of loss and regret over moving away from her parents and extended family.

Wendy realised that she deeply wanted her children to have a close relationship with their grandparents and the rest of her family.

When Wendy saw how and why she might come to regret her decision, she changed her mind and turned down the opportunity.

Her husband and kids were tremendously relieved to stay put and within a few months, an equally attractive offer in her local area was offered to Wendy.

Now, what about the feelings of guilt you experience when you want to do something nice for yourself, especially if it costs money or takes time?

Although I've seen women suffer over this more than men, it is by no means a women-only issue.

To find out whether this is 'good' guilt or 'bad' guilt, ask yourself the following questions:

- Will I regret doing this thing?
- Will I regret spending the time?
- Will I regret spending the money required to enjoy this delightful thing?"

If paying out all that money could cause a problem for you, don't do it.

However, often when you consider splurging on yourself, you do have the money and you do have the time - and yet 'bad' guilt stands in your way.

What do we know about this type of 'bad' guilt?

It's rubbish, right?

So, move on, pass go, and do this delicious thing!

You know you deserve it ☺

'Bad' guilt tends to place you in perpetual self-doubt, making you tortuously question your desires and motivations.

On the other hand, 'good' guilt feels more like a gentle nagging or prodding, asking you to do better for yourself and your life.

By identifying the source of your guilt - whether it's doing something you're liable to regret or if you're holding yourself to an impossible standard - you're likely to feel relief.

Your guilt may dissipate.

Whenever you feel ease melt over you or are surprised by experiencing elation, give yourself a pat on the back.

You've struck gold. You've connected with your wisdom.

## IS THAT YOUR INSPIRATION OR YOUR EGO SPEAKING?

Do you know when your desire to do something is stemming from ego gratification versus when it's truly responding to inspiration from within?

Working with people who want more out of their lives, I see how so many of us are deeply affected by the celebrity culture we live in.

Our idea of 'making it' usually involves a lot of the money and fame we see being lavished on entertainers and sports figures.

Now, nothing against thinking big, but this false vision of success can make it hard for us to set the goals and pursue the path that will truly fulfil us in life.

Such cultural brainwashing causes us to question ourselves if we aim for achievements that are less grand than total physical, emotional and financial perfection.

We often think that a big goal stems from inner inspiration, when it's really just an ego-motivated attempt to prove self-worth.

This doesn't mean that everyone who has the drive to achieve great things is doing so to be famous or is trying to validate self-worth by gaining stock in others' opinions.

It would however be interesting to see how many stardom seekers would still pursue their purported goals if there was little pay or recognition involved.

The few that would stick around are inspired - the rest are getting a need met.

I am not saying that the desire to be famous or making a lot of money is a 'bad' thing, I only mean to show you which feelings and inner motivations will help you attain ease and satisfaction.

This kind of thinking illustrates to us exactly what keeps us checking somewhere outside of ourselves for answers.

This can set us up to be a bottomless pit of need for external validation.

Hey, we're human, a need to external validation is going to happen once in a while, but you can save yourself a lot of strife if you learn to feel the difference between ego and inspiration.

When feelings of insecurity strike, keep in mind what ego feels like and what inspiration feels like.

Inspiration comes from within, and ego depends on others to feel at ease and satisfied.

Inspiration will always feel less tumultuous than ego.

# PASSION WILL ALWAYS ALLOW YOU TO GO THE EXTRA MILE

Beating a competitor, speaking in public, trying to take care of thirty items on your to-do list in a single day, coaching your child's football team to win against all odds - all these things make you feel charged up.

It's a temporary high that keeps you 'pumped up' and raring to go, but often leaves you empty and exhausted when the 'rush' dies down.

On the other hand, starting something from the ground up, losing track of time in the abandon of a project, stretching beyond what you feel capable of in the name of a good cause - these efforts can tire you as well, but here the exhaustion is more likely to resemble the satisfying weariness you experience after a long hike in the great outdoors. Much like writing this book has been for me, exhilarating yet all encompassing.

Of the two paragraphs above, the first describes activities fuelled by adrenaline; the second, activities fuelled by passion.

They key to distinguishing passion from adrenaline lies in understanding its source.

Remember, we are memorising feelings in order to hear the body's wisdom more clearly and act on what we feel.

What does boundless enthusiasm feel like?

What does an adrenaline rush feel like?

Which one is more sustainable?

Passion. An adrenaline rush lets you down hard and you need to muster another rush to sustain it.

Watching the ebb and flow of your energy will help distinguish between the two.

Adrenaline excites us - excitement makes us feel good - so we stick with it.

But when it comes down to relying on your body for wisdom clues, adrenaline will fool you every time. It causes you to feel such a rush that you could misinterpret it at any time.

Adrenaline lies.

It's a high that makes you feel bigger and more capable than you really are.

When you make decisions under the influence of an adrenaline rush, you are doing so based on short-lived feeling that could leave you frustrated down the road.

Caught up in the hormonal charge, you may over extend yourself, promise more than you can deliver, or say "yes" when you really mean to say "no".

We talked earlier about the way adrenaline can wear down our system and how its insidious nature makes it hard to decipher.

It feels like passion and excitement, but it isn't.

Donna's story will serve to illustrate this point.

# 'LYBL' STORY: ENTER DONNA

## LIVING ON AN ADRENALINE HIGH

**D**onna has been a mentor to me and is someone I have long admired.

She is someone who thrives on helping others. People seek her counsel or ask for her help on projects because she is known for possessing deep wisdom and insight, as well as for having the patience of a saint.

Donna came to me for coaching after battling breast cancer (having already battled thyroid cancer).

Although our main agenda was to build her small business, Donna's health was frequently addressed. She was often exhausted, but was unable to see how paying attention to the needs of others debilitated her.

In fact, Donna thought helping others propped her up. When she felt needed, her adrenaline kicked in and she would go on a high, spreading the fairy dust of her good will and saving the day whenever she could.

Through our coaching, Donna began to see she could be just as helpful to others without depleting her own energy. She learned that if she wanted to say no, she could. She realised that she was not ultimately responsible for everyone who wanted her help and that by saying no, she might actually end up being more helpful to these people in the long run by forcing them to help themselves.

As hard as it was, Donna admitted to needing the high she got from being needed.

She started to feel the difference between experiencing an adrenaline rush and a true desire to help someone else.

She re-evaluated the priorities in her life, separating adrenaline from genuine passion.

Yes, some people were disappointed when their 'saviour' wasn't readily available. But to this day, Donna remains cancer-free. She attributes this to learning how to say "no" to over promising, needing to be needed and adrenaline rushes.

# KNOW WHEN YOU ARE BEING SEDUCED

Have you ever been offered something that is too good to be true?

An incredible business opportunity, a free trip, an out-of-the-blue-invitation to attend a ritzy event?

When presented with opportunities like these, most of us will hear a small voice in the back of our minds asking, "What's the catch?"

That little voice is probably trying to get you to pay attention to another key distinction to watch for as you uncover your true 'wants'.

Often, something you want, such as saying "yes" to a seemingly great opportunity, is not a true opportunity, but rather a seduction.

The sooner you listen to that voice, the easier your life will be.

True opportunities benefit all parties involved – they are ecological.

You will feel a sense of ease and expanded possibility when presented with one.

A seduction, on the other hand, usually means that you get something out of it temporarily, but the party offering it to you benefits a lot more. You get used as the offeror's needs are met.

This sort of seduction usually does not feel free and unrestrained. You may sense tension or doubt about the other party's intentions.

When you can feel the difference between an opportunity and a seduction, you can prevent yourself from expending unnecessary energy in pursuit of a disappointing reward.

Your body's clues - the feeling that something is not quite right - is your natural wisdom speaking to you.

## 'LYBL' STORY: MEET JENNY & ROD

My client Jenny met Rod, a fellow consultant, at a conference.

Rod was looking for a new partner for a venture he was starting up. Although Jenny had a feeling immediately that he was not to be fully trusted, he also seemed genuine, informed, connected and savvy. Jenny ignored her misgivings because she could not point to any specific reason not to get involved with this man.

It took two years and a lot of legal paperwork to get Jenny out of that relationship.

Sadly, Rod's venture went bust.

Jenny lost time, money and a great deal of emotional energy in extracting herself from her professional relationship with him.

Despite our coaching, she had not been willing to trust what she ultimately knew was true until she had plenty of evidence that she had been seduced and not the recipient of an opportunity.

Unfortunately, by then, the damage had been done.

## IS IT JUST A PHASE YOU ARE GOING THROUGH?

Knowing the difference between certainty and infatuation is another subtle distinction that can help us come up with a clearer path to what we most want from our lives.

For me the word 'infatuation' always conjures up an intense schoolgirl crush, the kind that was unrelenting, all-encompassing and totally intoxicating.

A feeling and a stream of consciousness that consumes the days and nights, until you're unaware of anything else. What's wrong with that I hear you asking?

Nothing, I suppose - except it's just a big old waste of time and something you'll write off in the name of experience.

Certainty, on the other hand, is something you can take action on.

It dictates direction.

Although certainty is not completely concrete, it's better than indecision.

Let's stick to romantic relationships here for a moment, since I started talking about schoolgirl crushes. When you are infatuated with someone, your family and friends never seem to be wholeheartedly accepting of the relationship.

However, if you are certain you've found the love of your life, even when the others aren't as sure of your choice, they generally leave you to your own devices.

It doesn't mean they don't care enough to intercede, but rather that people feel awe at wisdom. Even if your family and friends can't see what you see in your beloved, they respect that there is something you know that they don't.

They are willing to respect your certainty, even if they would have seen through you if you'd merely been infatuated. It's easy for caring, objective bystanders to see through infatuation. It bothers them. Infatuation suggests an absence of sound judgment and people react to the insanity of this.

What does this all mean for your life's blueprint?

It's important for you to learn to feel the difference between infatuation and certainty.

If you are considering a new career opportunity in another city in a new state, ask yourself if it is the right job for you or whether you are infatuated with the idea of moving to a new city and starting again.

If you are thinking of starting your own business, ask yourself whether it is because you know with certainty that you want to be your own boss, with all the responsibility for the success or failure of the business, or if you are just in love with the idea of being able to say to people that you work for yourself.

Wow, so there you go, we've managed to look at only six subtleties. Now that you've learned to distinguish between them, some themes are starting to emerge.

Most of the less desirable feelings are based in fear or a perception of something missing.

The fear could be a fear of consequences or a fear of not having or being enough.

There will usually be an external measurement at the root of the fear and it will probably be emotionally 'noisy'. There would probably be a noticeable absence of peace, grace and ease, the signs that you've connected with your own wisdom.

A wisdom-based decision will never be dictated by fear.

You may have to overcome fear (which we talked about in Chapter 3), but the truth about what direction to take will always be rooted in courage, love, integrity and goodness.

The big questions will be:

Are you worth it?

Will you give it to yourself?

Will you do what you know is right for you?

# IT'S TIME TO GRAB YOUR 'LYBL' JOURNAL!

## 'LYBL' THROUGH WRITING

### Acknowledging Your Subtleties

Spend time writing down how you feel about the difference between 'good' and 'bad' guilt, inspiration and ego, passion and adrenaline, opportunity and seduction and certainty and inspiration.

You already wrote about the difference between 'want' and 'should' on Page 148.

Give specific reference to people, places and details that will remind you of times when you have felt these subtleties.

Record any lessons you have learned, and how you will recognise these feelings in the future.

When you pay more attention to how you feel in situations instead of relying on linear logical judgment, you will have quicker access to the answers that will make a difference in attaining what you want.

# BEING IN 'THE ZONE'

Once you have learned to identify these subtleties of feeling, you are ready to recognise the not-so-subtle feeling of entering 'the zone'.

In sports, 'the zone' is the place where athletes feel connected to a force that propels them to the perfect game.

They report an ease and a lack of effort, even though they are fully present in the moment. It's as if time stands still and the hyper-awareness of the moment creates a dreamlike state. In that suspended reality mind, body and spirit come together effortlessly to perform flawlessly.

That is a similar zone with wisdom and when you enter it for the first time, you have a physical feeling that things are right, as if the stars have aligned in your favour.

Your inner compass is pointing to true north.

You will always remember this feeling because it marks a moment when you put yourself on the course to your life blueprint.

You've entered the zone.

Wisdom is the zone of decision-making.

The feeling you are looking for is the same ease that the well-trained athlete can achieve. You become the well-trained player when you allow yourself to know how you feel.

When you enter the wisdom-zone, you may feel a lightness, as if all the heaviness of your life were dissipating. You may experience a feeling of expansion: your brain may feel as if it has expanded, your heart and lungs too.

Some of my clients have even described a feeling of having a new brain transplanted into their body, it is that obvious.

These are feelings of tapping into wisdom.

# 'LYBL' STORY: ENTER ANITA

## THE TRUTH ALWAYS FINDS A WAY

Anita was a client who worked in a large family business for many years. She liked her work, but felt that her talents were not fully used in this job and worse, her opinions were constantly lost in the family pecking order.

For a long time Anita had wanted to start her own business.

Through our work together, she was able to overcome her fear of upsetting her family by striking out on her own.

Anita endured near being disowned by her family and their harsh criticism.

Still, she felt a certain lightness about her decision that gave her confirmation that she was doing the right thing. It felt surreal, and she was amazed at her level of calm.

If she wanted to, she could conjure up as much turmoil as her family was experiencing, but she knew it wasn't what she was really feeling. Instead, Anita was in touch with a feeling of expansion and freedom that started in her solar plexus and reverberated through her body.

Anita has been successfully running her own business for more than two years now. She can still measure the feelings to know she is staying on track.

# COACHES WRAP UP

**I**n this chapter you learned how to get beyond your thoughts and let your feelings tell you what to do.

You saw how to:

- Continually take care of and eliminate what keeps you too busy to feel
- Keep your focus on how your priorities are reflected in your life
- Feel the difference between 'want' and 'should'
- Pay attention to subtleties in emotion: the distinctions between your wisdom and your coping mechanisms (inspiration vs. ego, passion vs. adrenaline, etc.)
- Be in 'the zone' and use it to know when your actions are wisdom based

# CHAPTER 5

# CREATE YOUR OWN
# PERSONAL MANIFESTO
# THE POWER OF NOW

So much of our life is geared toward future achievements and successes that it's often hard to remember it is the present we inhabit.

We are forced to be 'big girls' and 'big boys' before we are ready.

We are trained to think about University before we've finished our H.S.C - Higher School Certificate.

We are asked our thoughts on marriage and having babies before we've even dated someone for six months.

The list goes on, but the point is that our success is often measured by where we are headed instead of where we actually are.

Although there's nothing wrong with planning, visualising and looking ahead, many of us struggle to reach the future without really paying attention to what is going on in the present.

My clients most often come to me wanting to create a great future and they are often surprised to learn that the way to do this is by taking care of the present first.

We begin our work by facing the truth about what a client's life circumstances are telling her. If these are not what she wants them to be (and they usually are not), we then work diligently to change her life focus, re-examine her priorities and come up with solutions to her present-day problems.

Taking care of all these things releases a tremendous amount of negative energy, after which attracting a great future is easier.

# 'LYBL' STORY: ENTER DEBBIE

A personal training studio in Melbourne asked me to help one of its members, Debbie, to achieve the goal of getting in the best physical shape of her life.

She had been given a professionally designed exercise schedule and routine, but she was always too exhausted to follow this regime.

When we began working together, it was clear to me that she was hoping we could skip over the reality of the present (that she was exhausted) and magically get her into the best shape of her life.

Hhhhhmmmm.

Focusing on the present, Debbie and I discovered that she didn't leave the office until quite late every night. In addition, she did not eat well or drink enough water during the day, and she didn't get enough sleep.

To solve these challenges, we created an ideal schedule that allowed her time to include meals and adequate rest. It meant more delegating at work and being ruthless with her time.

I knew that Debbie's motivation and ability to change her future could develop only if she took better care of herself in the present.

It is just impossible to reach a future goal if the present is not set up to support it.

Yet we continue to waste our present in hope for a better future. "If only I had this (or that), things would be better'" we say. Or, "If I can just make some money to cover this credit card debt, then I'll be alright". Or, "when I find a partner, I'll be happy".

I truly learned the power of now throughout my journey with cancer.

Whatever the case may be for you, keep in mind that the fastest way out is through.

This chapter is about facing the truth and doing something about it.

The results may be even better than what you were spending your precious present moment wishing for.

For me, I earned the gift of life.

# WHAT IS A PERSONAL MANIFESTO?

Facing the truth and doing something about it involves making a pact with yourself that says you will do whatever it takes to make your life work in the present.

Call this pact a personal manifesto.

This manifesto means you are willing to give up big goals and fantasies of salvation in order to deal with what is true about your life now, and make it work.

Our job is to be an example of a life that is working.

A life that is working is one in which your complaints are at a minimum and, although everything may not be perfect, it works.

You have more than enough money, more than enough love and support, more than enough satisfaction out of the things that you do and the company you keep.

When you make a personal manifesto, you will start to by taking care of the 'real matters' at hand. These matters are those things that are not working for you on a daily basis. Those things could include a relationship that gives you trouble, finances that are less than stellar, a job you hate, or anything else that plagues you and doesn't seem to be resolving itself.

The personal manifesto does not apply to people in dire straits: it is useful for every single person who is not happy, regardless of his or her income level or social status.

Even people at the top of their game sometimes suffer from wishing it would all go away tomorrow. Such fruitless yearning can plague anyone who has neglected his or her own wisdom. The yearning may be a result of neglecting the signs that you need a change, a rest, a resolution to a problem or an antidote to the situation.

To make a personal manifesto with yourself, first look at all aspects of your life to determine what is working and what is not. This is not the time to dream big and desire for the ideal.

It is not the time to set goals.

It is the time to evaluate what is true for you right now.

Ask yourself:

What makes me happy?

My home?

My job?

My family?

What is not satisfying?

Do I want to be in better physical shape?

Do I want a better relationship with my parent, my spouse or my child?

Making a personal manifesto does not require that you have solutions to the less desirable elements of your life, just that you take stock of them.

# IT'S TIME TO GRAB YOUR 'LYBL' JOURNAL!

### TAKE STOCK: WHERE ARE YOU CURRENTLY AT?

Use this list to evaluate what works and what doesn't in your immediate world.

You will also find a copy of this list in your purchased copy of your LYBL Journal should you like to refer to it there.

Write 'yes' next to each item if you are satisfied with how it is working in your life, or 'no' if you are not satisfied.

If you are sometimes satisfied, write 'no' because there is probably some work for you to do on this item.

It may also help to ask yourself, "Does this work for me or against me?" and "Does it contribute positively to my life or negatively?"

Feel free to add any items I have not included that are relevant to you.

You will be instructed on what to do with this information later in this chapter.

| 'LYBL' IN ACTION<br><br>Evaluate Your Life | | | |
|---|---|---|---|
| **RELATIONSHIPS** | **YES / NO** | **ENVIRONMENT** | **YES / NO** |
| Spouse or partner | | Home | |
| Child/children | | Office | |
| Parents | | Outside view | |
| Siblings | | Car | |
| Friends | | Bedroom | |
| | | | |
| **POSSESSIONS** | | **HEALTH / WELLBEING** | |
| Clothes | | Emotional life | |
| Appliances | | Body | |
| Work tools | | Nutrition | |
| "Toys" | | Habits | |
| Furniture | | Indulgences | |
| | | | |
| **CAREER / WORK** | | **FINANCES** | |
| Culture/atmosphere | | Money management | |
| Co-workers | | Habits | |
| Workload | | Income | |
| Job description/ responsibilities | | Spending | |
| Purpose | | Savings | |
| Vision | | | |
| | | | |

| ACTIVITIES | | | |
|---|---|---|---|
| Social | | | |
| Spiritual | | | |
| Religious | | | |
| Leisure | | | |
| Volunteer | | | |
| School | | | |

# 'LYBL' STORY: ENTER MATTHEW

## BRINGING YOUR PERSONAL MANIFESTO TO LIFE

**M**atthew likes fast cars, fast women, fast deals and fast food - the faster, the better.

He considered himself a mover and a shaker.

By the outside world's standards, he was successful, but in private he admitted to me that he felt disconnected from others.

He wouldn't dream of letting anyone in his circle know how he felt, however, because he presumed he needed to keep up his image as a savvy, together guy.

Matthew had chosen to work with me to examine how he managed his life and to see how he could be more satisfied with the life he led.

Filling out the checklist above, Matthew recognised that first of all, he had to improve his eating habits and his physical health.

Due to his flamboyant lifestyle, he was out of shape and feeling sluggish.

He also found that he needed to pay more attention to how he dealt with money; since he was rapidly running up huge credit card debt.

Finally, it was clear he had to do some work on his relationships, because his conscience was bothering him.

Matthew made a personal manifesto, committing to take action on what was not working in his life and turn it around.

He began by reconciling some old relationships and mending some old hurts with past lovers. A great weight was lifted off him by doing so. He further increased his feeling of wellbeing by banishing junk foods from his diet and resuming exercise.

Clearing up his debts was a much slower process, but just knowing he was taking action toward doing so contributed to the increased vitality he felt.

Matthew experienced not just heightened energy but a sense of ease and increased peace of mind. He began to attract new and interesting people into his life, people who shared his new interests and healthier lifestyle. In turn, these new friendships brought a fresh set of possibilities and opportunities into his life.

Within just a few months, Matthew changed from a dissatisfied mover and shaker to someone who was enjoying a richer, more fully connected life on many levels.

He no longer cared to keep up a pretentious image.

He didn't have to.

His life was beginning to work and he no longer had to live a lie.

As his relationship with himself improved, so too did his relationship with money, because the more he valued himself, the more money he attracted and retained.

# LET TRUTH SET YOU FREE

When you make a personal manifesto, you have finally listened to the truth about the circumstances in your life and you have no choice but to take responsibility for them.

It takes so much energy to deny the truth and hide from it that once you admit to it, you feel an immediate release and burst of renewed positive energy.

The truth offers you wisdom (even when it isn't positive), because once the truth is spoken, you are free to take action.

You are free to change.

You are free to create forward motion in your life.

The tricky thing about the truth is that it is always changing.

Once spoken, what is true for you today could turn out to be no longer true tomorrow or the next day.

For example, if you share your feelings of hurt with a friend or co-worker whose words have wounded you, the hurt might disappear, just having spoken it.

Once you are no longer experiencing hurt, you are living a different truth.

Admitting what is true in a way that does not hurt others allows the possibility of a wise solution to or even the transformation of a negative situation.

One of my closest friends spent years denying he was bankrupt, living painfully cloaked in shame and deceit.

Once he admitted the truth of his circumstances to himself and the people around him, he discovered the consequences of declaring bankruptcy were not nearly as harsh as he had feared. He was then able to close down his business with dignity, speak to his creditors openly and begin a new and more resourceful life.

Our tendency is to avoid difficult truths, trying strategy after strategy to do so, only to be left feeling empty or frustrated. Even if we succeed in covering up our reality, it becomes an empty and hollow victory.

The underlying problem is still there.

When you make a personal manifesto and tell the truth about your life, you have allowed your life to tell you what it needs from you, instead of telling your life what you need from it.

When we are not satisfied with our lives, no matter how out-wardly perfect they look, this is what is going on.

We cannot override the truth.

No matter how hard we try, we cannot.

You can spend a lifetime trying, but in the end it will have been a much harder life.

Deal with what is true.

# 'LYBL' STORY: ENTER NATHAN

## FREEDOM & TRUTH RIDE TOGETHER

Nathan was an executive chef at a five-star hotel in Melbourne.

His company was grateful for his years of service, but he was concerned that he was not changing with the times.

Deep down, Nathan knew that his managers were growing impa-tient with him and his job was in danger if he did not make some changes, This truth, however, was very hard for him to face.

Nathan was a very proud man who at first found it hard to trust me with his private thoughts and struggles.

Once trust was established, it became clear to me that he treat-ed his staff very poorly, showing little patience, cultural sensi-tivity or faith in their ability to carry out his orders.

He micromanaged and basically ran the kitchen as a dictatorship.

He resisted becoming computer-literate, thus further hampering his effectiveness.

He worked ridiculously long hours, letting weeks pass before he would reluctantly take a day off. This put a tremendous strain on his relationships with his wife and seriously cut into the time he longed to spend with his young grandchild. The stress and isolation of his life was taking its toll, and after years of abstinence, he had started drinking again.

As hard as it was for Nathan to share these things with a stranger, he felt tremendous relief when, with my help, he made a personal manifesto.

Admitting his difficulties was enough to start improving.

Admitting he was drinking made him feel accountable enough to give up alcohol without additional help.

He asked one of his junior staff members to coach him on improving his computer skills and as a result was able to teach another staff how to do the ordering and accounting electronically.

Learning from someone his junior helped him gain respect for this young staff member, which in turn aided Nathan in slowly delegating responsibilities and giving instructions in a more empowering way.

In time, his kitchen became a well-run, friendly place.

Before committing to his personal manifesto, Nathan used to go home grumpy and was unable to engage in conversation that required problem solving or intimacy.

Now he was able to ask for the time he needed for himself to decompress.

He was now more equipped to engage with his loved ones in a way that fuelled their relationships. The new intimacy and peace he'd helped to create made home a place he looked forward to being and a place he enjoyed.

After a few months, Nathan was asked to be part of a launch team for several new hotels his company was building across the country.

All of Nathan's forward motion and improvement started only after he admitted the truth about his present and resolved to change it.

# YOU ALREADY HOLD THE ANSWERS

If you are like most of the people I have worked with, you already know what needs to change in your life.

You don't need me to tell you, any more than do my clients, who simply can't bring themselves to make the necessary changes or have convinced themselves they don't know how to make them.

I hold the belief that everyone I meet is already whole and complete.

And they are, you all are.

And by now, you've taken a good hard look at what is working in your life and what is not.

I trust that you've been able to be truthful with yourself during this process.

All you need is a little push to get you towards doing something that you've discovered.

# IT'S TIME TO GRAB YOUR 'LYBL' JOURNAL!

## 'LYBL' THROUGH WRITING

### You Already Know What Needs To Be Done

This activity will show you how you already know what needs to be done in your life.

Return to the checklist in which you identified the areas in your life that were and weren't working for you.

In your LYBL Journal, create a separate page or heading for each area in the checklist: relationships, environment, possessions, health and wellbeing, career/work, finances and activities.

Focus on the aspects in each group that you have already determined are not working.

For each item, ask yourself the following 'LYBL QUESTIONS':

- "What do I need to know about solving my issues with my........?" (e.g. finances, relationships, etc.)
- "What do I need to do about my..........?" (e.g. environment, activities etc.)

Pose each question, take a deep breath and then write down the answer spontaneously.

Don't think too much about your response.

Frame your answers as if the issues themselves were speaking to you.

For example, if you are having a challenge in a particular relationship, respond to the question as if you were the person with whom you are having the problem.

It might sound like this: "What you need to know is that I'm sorry I broke your trust. What you need to do is forgive me." Or if your savings plan is not working, your money itself may speak: "What you need to do is save 10 per cent of every week's salary."

When you have finished, go back and use a highlighter to mark things that translate into direction action items.

For example, if your money told you. "It's time to invest", highlight those words.

Then, make a list of action items from each heading.

These lists become part of your personal manifesto.

These are the simple goals and actions that will matter in excavating the blue print for your best life.

# THE ONLY WAY OUT IS THROUGH

Commit now to doing whatever it takes to be responsible in every area of your life.

This is, of course usually easier said than done.

I suggest you start by concentrating only on one area, and don't go on to tackle another until you are ready.

Be compassionate with yourself.

By this, I'm not saying you should be lazy, just that you need to be kind to yourself as you deal with the challenges of perfecting your present.

Remember, the only way out is through.

This is why we did all that work on understanding what you're feeling in the last chapter.

When you can feel the truth, you can tell it and once it's told, action must be taken.

Nothing clears the way to your best life faster than doing the immediate work that your life requires.

There are no short cuts.

To me, the following story (which a friend sent to me) perfectly illustrates this.

## Words of Wisdom: Leaving the Moth to Do the Work

A man found a cocoon of an emperor moth and took it home to watch the moth emerge. One day, a small opening appeared in the cocoon and he watched as the moth struggled to force its body through that tiny hole.

After several hours though, it seemed to stop making progress, as if it had got as far as it could and could go no further.

It was stuck.

Then the man decided to help the moth, so he took a pair of scissors and snipped off the remaining bit of cocoon. This allowed the moth to emerge easily. But it had a swollen body and small, shrivelled wings.

While the man continued to watch the moth, expecting its wings to enlarge and expand at any moment to be able to support its body, this never happened.

The little moth spent the rest of its life crawling around with a swollen body and shrivelled wings.

It was never able to fly.

What the man, in his kindness, did not understand was that the restricting cocoon and the struggle required for the moth to get through the opening were nature's way of forcing fluid from the body of the moth into its wings, so that it would be ready for flight once it achieved its freedom from the cocoon.

Freedom and flight could come only after the struggle.

By depriving the moth of a struggle, he deprived the moth of health.

How many times have we wanted to take the quick way out of struggles, to take scissors and snip off our difficulties in order to be free of them?

How many times have we wanted to do this for our kids, loved ones and colleagues?

We need to remember, however, that it is through our trials and struggles that we are strengthened, for it is in these things that we learn the lessons that we need to in life.

# 'LYBL' STORY: ENTER JOANNE

### YOUR FUTURE STARTS NOW

Joanne, a photographer, always had money problems.

She tended to make promises in her business she couldn't keep, and her unhappy clients would refuse to pay her. Joanne would then borrow from family and friends, but be unable to repay her debts. She often resorted to lying and cheating to get by.

I never officially worked with Joanne as a client, so I could only watch from the sidelines, so what I saw was remarkable.

One day, she decided to get her life in order.

She did so in very small steps, fighting her natural tendencies all the way.

Despite her efforts to arrive on time, be diligent about her work, and finally open a bank account to keep track of her money, life soon began to test her resolve.

Joanne lost her wallet and had to chase down all the pieces of her life.

She got kicked out of her flat for her previous habits of not paying rent and had to move in with a friend.

Many people were sick of her antics and did not believe she had changed.

Although they turned their backs on her, she did not falter. She worked to save money and contribute to her friend's household expenses.

She had finally decided to deal with what was true in her life and grow from it instead of dishonouring herself by avoiding it.

After a year, Joanne rented her own living space and began to see her reputation as a photographer rise again.

She mended some of her old friendships and paid off her debts. It took a few more years before she felt on top of her finances and began to breathe easily again.

Even though she would be the first to tell you that she would have been heading for disaster if she had not decided to face reality, she is grateful for the accomplishment of being able to say she turned her own life around.

Joanne did this by admitting the truth and doing the work to turn around what she had done step by little step.

To escape from the whirlwind that had become her life, she had to lower her expectations and make her focus very narrow and simple.

In effect, she made a personal manifesto and it began with keeping her word.

# STAY TRUE TO YOUR PROMISES

Telling the truth about your life's circumstances is only one part of your personal manifesto.

Keeping your word once you've given it is also a critical component of the contract.

Keeping your word means staying true to promises you make, especially to yourself.

Believe it or not, we tend to betray ourselves even more than we do others.

It is to ourselves that we must first begin to give our word and keep it.

This means not only telling the truth, but also learning to make promises that we can keep in the first place.

Having faith, or trust, in ourselves is absolutely essential to anything we want to accomplish in life. We lose that trust every time we do not keep a promise to ourselves.

If you broke as many promises with a small child as you do with yourself, you would not be surprised if the child didn't trust you and walked on eggshells around you.

Similarly, breaking your own promises to yourself erodes your self-esteem.

It deafens you to your own innate wisdom.

Whatever you neglect to honour - the promise to work out, eat well, save money, spend less, be more patient or play with your kids more, or any other vow that matters to you - these betrayals of self, and the associated guilt and shame we often feel, become an undetectable poison under our skin.

The fact is, although we live the false sense that the core of our worldly success is our goals and being better and smarter, the true work is being able to trust ourselves implicitly.

When you do this, you have confidence in yourself, confidence that shines through and acts as a beacon for success.

The secret to keeping your promises is to simplify.

Make your every promise small enough to be do-able.

Don't make an all-encompassing promise that all but sets you up for failure.

Instead of saying, "I won't eat anything fattening today" say, "I will keep my word to watch my nutrition today and make conscious choices about what I eat".

You can still choose to blow your daily intake on an ice cream cone, but you do so consciously.

Instead of saying, "I won't raise my voice at work anymore," say "I will keep my cool today" - or for the next hour, or what time period is short enough so that you can keep your promise to yourself.

Small promises allow you to be someone of your word.

Your word is the glue that holds your best life together, and every broken promise to yourself is a crack in the foundation that supports your life.

If you don't keep promises you will not be punished or suffer some grave fate, it will simply make it harder for you.

You may not be conscious of where you are breaking promises, so if you feel life does not trust you as you'd like, take a look at where you are not keeping your word.

Then start keeping your word, or simplify what you promise so you can keep it.

# PAY ATTENTION TO YOUR LIFE

In order for you to make and keep the personal manifesto, you'll also need to become the observer of it. Just as an actor would observe someone to portray them, observing your life allows you to live in it fully.

In his book, The E-Myth, Michael Gerber describes how a business owner, in order to be most successful must work not only in his business but also work on his business.

As your coach, I ask you to do the same for your life.

You can't just be in your life, you must work on it.

To do this, take the time to pay attention to your life instead of just surviving each day.

Your world is giving you feedback and clues that you need to stop to observe.

It is showing you the way, and any obstacles are part of that journey.

By observing your life as if you were outside it, you accelerate positive changes because you learn more quickly about yourself and your life.

To observe your own life requires learning how to be an observer of all life.

It also requires some of the detachment (not taking things personally) that we explored in Chapter 3.

You must step back and take cues from the work around you.

# Words of Wisdom: Look To Nature For Lessons

When we study nature, what is it that we learn?

Let's take trees for example.

Trees instinctively grow towards the sky.

They also have long lives and the resilience to stand their ground, literally and figuratively through all kinds of weather.

Deep roots surely have something to do with it.

In essence, trees are the quintessential servants, creating oxygen for all to breathe, and apart from the carbon dioxide that we breathe out, they ask for nothing in return.

From trees, surely we can learn the need to be sure of ourselves and to serve others as well.

There is so much wisdom to be learned through the observations of trees that can be used in life.

You too, can learn much about yourself and your life through this one simple aspect of nature.

What else can you draw upon from nature?

**O**bserving life doesn't mean you sit in the spectator's booth watching it pass you by.

It means you are willing to learn from everything around you.

It means you are willing to not have the answers, willing to ask for help, willing to do whatever it takes to make your life work and willing to marvel at the results.

Being the observer of your own life gives you the perspective that can cause a level of recognition and awareness that may very well trigger a quantum leap in what you can accomplish.

For example, after I wrote my first book 'Bringing Life to Leadership', I knew that I instantly had to write my next book, the one that you are reading now, however I was stuck on how to present my ideas to share with the world.

There are so many ways to frame how coaching affects people's lives and with many other people already writing about it, I was challenged as to how to make it unique and useful.

The more I pondered it, the less I seemed to have an answer.

When I finally pulled back and observed, I allowed myself to have the answer.

I watched myself as I worked; I watched my clients, I studied their lives and the results they got from our work together and in their lives as a result.

I also carried in my heart all of you, the people who would read this book and focused on what was the message I felt you needed to hear to truly live your best life.

Suddenly, what I needed to do became clear.

My role in writing this book was to help others access their own wisdom that they already have within them that was designed to lead them to opportunity and satisfaction.

With amazing speed, wisdom flew to the top of everything I wrote, to the point this this book tripled in its intended length, because things just started flowing out of me at a rapid rate of knots.

Clients, mentors, family and friends responded with such enthusiasm that it became undeniable that our innate inner wisdom simply had to be the focus of this book.

The speed and momentum I experienced in making this decision is what I mean by quantum leaps. It can happen to you too, if you stand back and observe your life for a moment or two.

# IT'S TIME TO GRAB YOUR 'LYBL' JOURNAL!

## 'LYBL' IN ACTION

### Observe Your Own Life

Use the next day of your life as a chance to observe your own life and life in general.

Keeping TV, radio and other noisy distractions to a minimum, for the next twenty-four hours, try the following:

- Don't pipe in at every conversation
- Daydream a little
- Watch your kids or other kids play (or fight)
- Notice nature

- Study human behavior (yours or someone else's)
- Let other people 'win', just be an observer

When the day is done, see what impressions are left on you.

Write down the answers to these questions:

- What did I learn?
- Did I notice anything I wouldn't have if I hadn't been trying?
- Was there an 'A-HA' moment? If so, what was it?
- Did anything in particular stand out?
- Did I notice my actions more, or those of others?
- What insights did I have about life or myself in general?
- As the observer did I help to see my world differently or more clearly?

Allow your realisations to flow freely and float them to the surface.

Notice the difference your acknowledgement of the realisations, feels within your body.

Notice the things you are now telling yourself.

# COACHES WRAP UP

**Y**our personal manifesto is the crux of 'Your Actions', a step that cannot be skipped in the process of living your best life.

It will help you get to a point where your life works, even at the simplest level, where goal setting and daydreaming become pleasurable games instead of desperate odysseys in search of self-worth.

Self-worth reveals itself readily once you keep your commitments to your very own personal manifesto.

'Righting' every area of your life, admittedly, has to take some work on your part.

I trust that you know you can find any information you need.

Get on the Internet, buy some of the books, hire a coach, or ask a friend.

Just like the humour mentors we talked about earlier in this book, look for people who can mentor you on the life area you are not strong in.

People are the vehicle by which our success comes to us.

Ask, ask, and ask. Asking for guidance or help is like telling the truth.

It releases you from the strain of the lie.

Just do it!

Let's review the steps to creating and honouring your personal manifesto:

- Focus on the present, not the future
- Draw on the power that now brings
- Tell the truth in order to determine what is working and what is not working
- Make a personal manifesto to 'clean up' everything in your life that does not work
- Do the work
- Keep your word to yourself
- Become the observer of your own life and learn from it

# CHAPTER 6

# DISCOVER & REVEAL YOUR
# OWN SELF-WORTH

**W**hat do you do?

It seems as though every conversation with a new acquaintance gets to this question sooner or later - usually sooner.

Whether you work at home or in an office, whether you bring in no income for your daily efforts or can boast a seven-figure salary, the topics of 'what you do' is inescapable in our culture.

To put it another way, when was the last time someone asked, "Who are you?, What is your unique purpose in this world?"

When we talk about making our life work, as we did in the last chapter, how we earn a living and what we are meant to do with our lives is bound to come up for examination.

Ours is a 'doing' culture.

We identify ourselves by our accomplishments and by how much doing (or not) we can squeeze into a day. We pass that attitude on to our kids as we encourage them to commit to an abundance of lessons, team sports, clubs, play and other activities.

We are not necessarily flawed by being part of a doing culture, and no-one can blame us for taking a heavy bite out of life.

However, being in constant motion can cause us to take the more physically tiring route to personal satisfaction.

This chapter is about learning to get better at defining ourselves by who we are, rather than by what we do.

Defining ourselves in this way makes it easier to manage being part of a doing culture.

More importantly, our doing becomes more significant.

This shift - from getting our identity from what we do, to getting it from who we are - is a big step toward the unfolding of the life we truly desire.

## WHAT'S YOUR PURPOSE?

I can't think of a single person I know who has not asked herself why she is here, what her purpose is, or what she can uniquely contribute to this world to make it a better place.

For some people, it's just a matter of wondering how to fill their days with something besides routine obligations and mundane chores.

Others are more concerned with meaningful self-expression.

Towards this goal, some of us volunteer in our communities, some work at influential careers and others feel raising children well is their best contribution.

But, despite our best intentions, so many of us still don't quite feel fulfilled.

We spend the majority of our waking hours working in one way or another, but we don't feel rewarded for our efforts.

We spend more time and mental and physical energy on that portion of our lives than anything else, and we make the mistake of giving more time to what we 'do' to find an ever elusive payoff.

Whether you are a workaholic corporate type or a stay-at-home parent, I would bet that your working hours are disproportionate to your off-duty time.

The truth is, most of us suffer to make a living and that is a waste of our potential.

Even with all the choices we have today, polls show that half of us would change our careers if given the chance.

A pay cheque is not enough anymore - we want to make a difference.

We want to know what we do matters.

We just need a little help to make us realise that we can have both, that we can trade in our less-than-satisfying work for deeply fulfilling work.

We all have the ability to live out what I call our lucrative purpose.

To discover and reveal your own self-worth.

Identifying your lucrative purpose can bring great clarity to the focus of your life, allowing you to experience a fullness and satisfaction that does not depend on effort, long-range planning, goal setting, goals accomplishing or financial gain.

It is the identification and recognition of who you are that can lead to the all-important impact on the world that you crave.

Your lucrative purpose is already imprinted on your soul; it's part of your life blueprint.

Once it is recognised, responding to your lucrative purpose requires acceptance of its existence and commitment to its good use.

At a recent seminar I was running, a Queensland woman stood up and said, "I have always identified myself by what I did. I was a business banking account manager, but I'd grown to hate it and have felt very lost as to what I'm supposed to do with my life"

I asked her what she felt her greatest natural ability was and she replied, "Helping other people in getting a task done."

As these words left her mouth, she realised this innate talent of hers could be of use in many other potentially satisfying careers.

"I am not limited by being a business banker" she said. "I can assist in so many different industries to make money - the possibilities are endless!"

What I saw here was someone who shifted the importance of being an assistant from what she did to who she was. She enjoys assisting, is fulfilled by it, and does not have to limit where or how she acts as an assistant.

Over the years of working with clients, I have noticed that when people get a sense of their natural abilities in terms of who they are instead of what they do, they naturally begin to feel a sense of purpose that allows them to turn their work into something they love by making minimal changes.

They easily become enthusiastic about what they do.

Since they are excited about their work and feel useful, they are making a huge contribution and they feel fulfilled whilst also earning a living.

Though I call this your lucrative purpose, it applies to your life in a much larger context than simply making a living.

'Lucrative' describes not only financial wealth but the other riches that you can obtain, such as a sense of well-being, an abundance of love and support in your life, an awe at the coincidences that show up to take care of your needs, or the satisfaction of knowing you make a difference in the world.

It is this kind of lucrative income that distinguishes the happy-go-lucky garbage man from the miserable millionaire executive.

Honouring what is innate and inherent to you is the easiest path to a sense of purpose and satisfaction.

And remaining truthful to your lucrative purpose is possible no matter what job you hold.

Initiating more projects, sharing your opinions and ideas more readily and redesigning your schedule, all with a focus on what you do best and your purpose, heighten your vitality.

I often get asked as to how I bring such a consistent flow of energy to all that I do, this is why!

Whatever you do becomes more enjoyable.

Whether you choose to commit your lucrative purpose to being the means by which you earn your keep, or you decide to make it just one part of your daily life, your lucrative purpose has the potential to move your life to unexpected places and even monetary gain.

# IT WILL OCCUR NATURALLY

Often I have heard people - especially women - say that others are always coming to them with their problems.

Many people describe this as a draining part of their lives and wonder why it would be so negative if it were truly their purpose.

Having others rely on you for constant help can sap a vital energy you need to keep focused on yourself.

A true lucrative purpose is vitalising, not draining.

In this case, if it energises you to help other people, great.

However, if the way you are constantly giving to others is not energising, you may need to put some limits on who you help and how you can help them.

Another stumbling block when people search for their lucrative purpose is that they often feel it must be a grand purpose in the world's eyes.

A woman at a recent talk I gave said, "I want to be Mother Teresa or somebody". I so appreciated her honesty in expressing her feeling that if her calling or purpose were not grand or holy, it wasn't 'right' or good enough, and, therefore, would not be fulfilling.

I know so many people who want to do or be something huge to benefit humankind and then suffer a lack of personal fulfilment because they can't even take one small step towards this enormous goal.

"Remember," I told this woman, "Mother Teresa did not become Mother Teresa by anointing masses all at once. She started with one sick man, whom she took home when no hospital would have him. She became a symbol of selfless caring by ministering to one person at a time. You don't have to save the world, just be your version of Mother Teresa, everyday, to everyone you encounter. Start with yourself, and then your dog, and see where that takes you."

We all need to listen and act on such advice, myself included.

The evolution of lucrative purpose may land you somewhere grand, it is however not about the grand goals, it is about simply living daily with your lucrative purpose in mind that will lead you in the end to fulfilment.

If following your lucrative purpose leads you to something huge, this will occur naturally - you won't have to force it.

It will be the result of your true achievement: discovering your lucrative purpose.

# YOUR MISSION OF SELF DISCOVERY

There are three steps to uncovering your lucrative purpose:

1. Recognising who you are for other people – what purpose they see you fulfilling in their lives.
2. Dissecting the true meaning of your dreams and aspirations. Your long-held dreams may lead to a slightly different reality from what you have expected.
3. Picking up the clues from your world that reflect these dreams and aspirations. Those who know and love you may hold the wisdom to point you to your lucrative purpose.

Let's look at each of these steps in turn.

It may help you to think of them not as linear steps but as 'light switches', three different ways that may offer the key to unlocking your lucrative purpose.

Explore each one to determine which speaks to you most clearly.

# LIGHT SWITCH # 1:

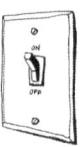

# IT'S NOT WHAT YOU'VE DONE, IT'S WHO YOU'VE BEEN

**W**hen charting a course for our futures, we often resort to figuring out what we can do next by following the example of what we have done in the past.

We'll look at our resumes, training, degrees, qualifications or experience and determine what work would match our profile. The past is a good place for career inspiration, but I believe you're looking at the wrong part of the past.

Don't look at what you've done; look at what you've been.

- What have employers and co-workers come to rely on you for?
- What have the people in your life naturally come to you for?
- How have people utilised you? Who have you been for them?
- Have people come to you because they needed a listener, or needed to solve a problem?

- Have people come to you to inspire creative ideas or model successful risk-taking?

Back when I worked in hospitality, my co-workers included aspiring talent of all kinds: actors, singers, clothing designers, would-be restaurateurs, electricians, students, musicians and so on.

What we had in common was that we were all stopping here only temporarily, as we aimed for other things.

Invariably, at some time or another, every one of my colleagues sat me down and asked me to help as each orchestrated plans to achieve desired goals. Even back then, I was always helping others see the forest instead of the trees.

I always wondered, "Why me? Why do people ask me to help when they are trying to reach a goal?"

It's only in hindsight that I understand that I was the guide for these people, someone who ushered them toward their desires.

Even further back in my life, I had been in a support group for students at University and would find myself doing the same thing for them.

This also carried over to the oncology ward when I was living my life with cancer.

To all these people, I was not so much a 'fellow bar manager', 'aspiring coach', or even 'enforcer of fun, support and guidance in the oncology department', they saw me as a guide to their goals and dreams.

My natural path - my lucrative purpose - was being laid even then.

Marlo Morgan's *'Mutant Message Down Under'* describes an Aboriginal tribe in the outback of Australia whose members are named not by a given name and a surname as Westerners traditionally use.

Instead, people are designated by the function they serve in the tribe: memory keeper, peacemaker, cook, medicine man, kin to birds, female healer, and the elder.

Each person's role was who he or she was.

A name changed only when the person developed a new role, and when that new purpose for that person emerged, the individual celebrated a birthday.

If we all honoured and valued ourselves in this way, ours would be a very different world.

# 'LYBL' STORY: ENTER GREG

### WHO ARE YOU REALLY?

Greg, who works in the biotech field, recently shared his story at a seminar of mine.

Upon recognising how people used him and how he got the most satisfaction out of his life and work, Greg started telling people he was a master motivator.

He stopped using his job title or any other label that described what he 'did'.

Just before making this discovery of his innate purpose, Greg had become dissatisfied at his job and started looking for a new position.

However, once he put his finger on his purpose, he pulled back the effort on his job search because he had a feeling that if he focused on this discovery, the perfect job would find him. (Smart guy!).

Greg altered the emphasis of his efforts at his current job so that what he did centred primarily around being a motivator of others.

One day, he went to an industry golf event.

Asked by one of the players in his tournament what he did, he told the man he was a master motivator.

As it turned out, his golf partner was the director of another company.

This man was so impressed with the positive energy coming from Greg that he offered him a chance at the perfect job before the round was over.

Greg did indeed get the job doing more of what he loved for a lot more money than he was making before - all because he identified his lucrative purpose.

# IT'S TIME TO GRAB YOUR 'LYBL' JOURNAL!

## 'LYBL' THROUGH WRITING

### Light Switch # 1 to Your Lucrative Purpose

It's your turn to approach your first light switch to your lucrative purpose.

Think back over your life and see if you can find a common thread in how people have utilised you.

Ask yourself:

- What have people always come to me for? Advice? Guidance? Education? A loan? A helping hand? Comforting?
- Who have I been for people? A truth-teller? A disciplinarian? A catalyst? An instigator? A voice of reason?

- What role do I play most often: The teacher? The nurturer? The leader? The risk-taker? The maverick? The motivator? The soother? The peacemaker?

Write your ideas down in your LYBL journal.

Do any of your findings surprise you?

Do you notice a consistent thread running through your past, have people pretty much always treated you the same, or have your roles changed?

Has your lucrative purpose made itself known?

# LIGHT SWITCH # 2:

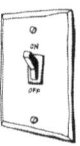

# THE TRUTH INSIDE YOUR DREAMS

Dreams can be a window to the soul.

Yet how many of us have had our dreams become our nightmares?

We sometimes stop using our unfulfilled visions as a form of inspiration and use them instead as a bat to beat ourselves with.

We see our unrequited dream as a broken promise to ourselves, or a goodness that life has cheated us of.

Yes, for some of us the dream to be a teacher, business executive or athlete was precisely the first step in pursuing and accomplishing the career goal.

For others of us that dream was only a metaphor or a clue that we did not know how to decipher.

Breaking that code is what I call discovering the truth inside your dreams, the essence of the dream.

This is the second light switch for revealing your lucrative purpose.

Discovering the essence of the dream means uncovering the most tangible parts of your dreams, which usually have to do with how your dreams serve others.

# 'LYBL' STORY: ENTER CATHY

Cathy once told me of her dream of one day owning her own flower shop, where she could create unique and unusual designs. In real life, she had no desire to work for another florist.

Her dream was having her own shop. It was that or nothing.

When I asked Cathy to tell me the essence of her dream, she said it was to brighten people's lives through flowers and beauty.

I pointed out that this was something she could do right then.

She didn't need to wait for an elusive 'one day' when she might have the financial resources to set up her own business.

Understanding the essence of her dream allowed this woman to shift her focus from the shop she didn't have.

Instead, she began to seek ways she could fulfil the essence of her dream here and now.

She did this by making a flower arrangement for a sick friend, who displayed the creation in her home. When her other friends came by they asked about the piece. These enquiries led to more business.

Eventually, Cathy's reputation grew enough that a local florist asked her to work for him. Over time, it was obvious that she was responsible for a lot of their repeat business, so a partnership arrangement was made.

In the end, she chose not to go off and start her own business.

She enjoyed the partnership and camaraderie she had developed.

By keeping her eyes on the essence of her dream, she achieved what she truly wanted.

If she'd ignored the clues within the dream and focused only on its literal meaning, she would still be seeking true fulfilment today.

To Cathy's story, let me add my own experience to show you how much you can gain from understanding the essence of your dreams. Throughout my teenage years, I was passionately pursuing my dream to be a nurse.

At one of my careers interviews, whereby I was being assessed for my suitability and to be accepted for the Diploma of Applied Health Science (Nursing) at Newcastle University, I was asked at the final interview, "What is possible if you become successful as a nurse?" My answer managed to get me accepted: "When I succeed as a nurse, it will mean that people will see me as a conduit to assist them to change their life, to make their world a better place. And if I really succeed at it and become well-known and respected, I will be a voice for change within the industry."

It was only ten years later that the full impact of that question became evident.

As I was struggling to find my direction in life, I remembered my answer and realised being a nurse was only one form of how the essence of my dream could be expressed.

Deep down, what I wanted was to have a positive impact on people's lives and help them make changes that would result in their happiness

It is no accident that the man who granted me acceptance into the course became my first coach years later and ushered me into the profession that expresses the essence of my dream completely.

# IT'S TIME TO GRAB YOUR 'LYBL' JOURNAL!

## 'LYBL' IN ACTION

### Finding The Essence Of Your Dream

After attending one of my retreat programs, a woman wrote to me:

*"For years I have struggled with not coming even close to living an unrequited passion of mine. I have always dreamed of becoming an art teacher and it has plagued me that I have never done anything about it. My life has not afforded me that opportunity and I've got sidetracked taking care of reality. I have not even taken steps towards it, so why do I suffer over it?*

*It is only now after having attended your 3-day event, and hearing you speak, that I finally understood what the dream was trying to tell me. Being a teacher of art is about bringing out the creative expression in people. This is something that I do in my current work and I can find many avenues to do. Thank you, thank you for the freedom*

*I have now found within and that I feel I now have. I don't have to feel depressed about this anymore. I am free!"*

Do you have an unfulfilled dream?

Is there something that you aspire to now or did aspire to at one time?

I'd like you to take a moment to write about your dream, if you have one, in your LYBL Journal.

Ask yourself the following questions:

- What is possible if you achieve, or had achieved, your dream? If you answer something like "I'd be rich" or "I'd be happy", then your reason is a creation from your head instead of your heart. Ignore it, and move deeper.
- How would other people benefit if you reached your dream?

Write down your answers and examine them closely.

They may very well contain the true essence of your dream.

You will know you have uncovered a clue as to what you are built to do when you latch onto something in your answers that:

- Is something you can start doing right away, such as, in my correspondent's e-mail example above, helping others express themselves creatively

> • Is something that had to do with how your gifts relate to other people. The woman in the example saw that she was meant to nurture the talents of others.
>
> As you do this exercise and hit upon the essence of your dream, spend some time thinking about how this translates into your lucrative purpose.
>
> Record your thoughts in your LYBL Journal.

What I want for you is that your dream no longer be a nightmare.

If your answer to "What is possible if you achieve your dream?" does not have the two characteristics mentioned above, it will represent a painful ride.

If by doing the coaching exercise you discovered that your dreams were more of a creation from your head instead of your heart ("I'd be rich", "I'd be happy", or "I'd be loved"), you may be experiencing a lot of stress and struggle due to the fact that these answers are all products of unmet needs - to be loved, to be heard, or approved of, or taken care of.

These needs surface and take hold because of what your child-hood may or may not have provided.

They will not prevent you from living your best life, but you'll need to make some adjustments to experience ease and to connect with your lucrative purpose.

The next story shows you what I mean.

# 'LYBL' STORY: ENTER RACHEL

### PUT YOUR PURPOSE TO ACTION: DON'T FALL PREY TO YOUR UNMET NEEDS

Rachel was as grounded in the action aspect of life as anyone could be. She was driven and highly successful and had a great partner, a great house, the right cars, a successful social life and all the trappings of success.

She started working with me because she had begun to recognise that her so-called success was taking a toll on her health and her personal life.

A highly rewarded and much applauded salesperson, Rachel had the dream of beating all the sales records at her company. Breaking many of them didn't seem to satisfy her so I asked her to tell me what would be possible for her if she succeeded at her dream.

"I'd be on top", she answered. "I'd win. I'd beat everyone else".

While this was the truth for her it did not fit the criteria for finding her lucrative purpose.

"Beating everyone else" was not something that could be put into effect immediately and it had nothing to do with serving other people.

Rachel's unmet need to win more than anything else was like a starving monster; it was never satisfied with what it got and always wanted more. Rachel was on a treadmill of winning, being dissatisfied with her winning, and starting all over again.

Rachel went back to her first light switch to explore finding her lucrative purpose and was dismayed by the recognition of who she had been to other people on the job.

Always competing, Rachel had been an antagonist to everyone she worked with.

She realised the power she had to have an impact on people and that she was not making the kind of impact she wanted to be known for.

Financially and emotionally, Rachel was not in the position to leave her taxing job.

However, she saw that in the meantime she could make her job easier by putting her energy toward finding and living her purpose instead of falling prey to the unmet needs that had been driving her.

She re-evaluated who she wanted to be to other people and decided to have an impact on all those she met in a way that supported them, rather than taking from them, as she had done in the past.

This was Rachel's lucrative purpose.

In working toward it at her current job, she so altered how she interacted with people that she was soon offered a new position, heading a team in a different department, and earned the same salary for working fewer hours with less stress.

Soon thereafter, Rachel discovered that she wanted to put her new people skills to work by becoming a coach and empowering others. She began her coach training with the same determination she had applied to her lucrative purpose, and she now uses coaching daily in her work and her life.

By simply putting your purpose into action, it would appear as if luck has come and seemingly picked you up and put you into a job or situation that best uses your gift.

When you unlock the wisdom of your dream, your best life cannot help but find you.

If you are in a work or life situation you hate, stop wasting your energy hating it and start being who you need to be to other people.

Unlock the essence of whatever dream teases you today and you will be released from that situation with little struggle from you.

Change your focus and take action.

# LIGHT SWITCH # 3:

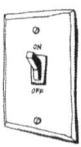

# LOOK TO THE PEOPLE AROUND YOU FOR YOUR CLUES

Throughout these pages, I've encouraged you to listen to yourself and ignore the assumptions and expectations of others.

In the name of finding your lucrative purpose, this is one place where I am inviting you to listen to what others say.

The final light switch that could uncover your lucrative purpose is through the clues that may have been thrown into your path by other people.

We've already established that your true purpose is found by who you are to others and/or how the essence of your dream serves them.

However, there is still more wisdom to be gleaned from those who know you and love you.

Sometimes, when you are unable or unwilling to hear your own wisdom, your friends may be shouting it at you.

Have you ever had several people say you would be well suited to a specific career or trade?

232

Well-meaning friends, relatives, colleagues, even strangers, are sometimes moved to make comments like "You should be a model" or "You'd make a great lawyer".

Often, we brush off such statements as trivial compliment, but perhaps we should learn to take heed.

If you have been hearing the same theme over and over from different people, maybe it's time to pay attention. Others may not exactly be pointing out the perfect road for you, but what they are seeing may reflect a clue as to what would really bring you joy in life.

For example, a teacher is someone who facilitates learning for others. If people have seen you as a potentially good teacher, this doesn't necessarily mean you're meant to be in a classroom. This could apply to whatever you are doing now, such as giving a presentation in your current job or mentoring someone on your team.

It could be that you are supposed to merely raise the volume on using your teacher-like talents and see where that leads you.

Listening to others is another way of letting your world speak to you, instead of demanding answers all the time from your circumstances.

The people around you are reflecting you.

How they do so gives you yet another way of uncovering your lucrative purpose.

# IT'S TIME TO GRAB YOUR 'LYBL' JOURNAL!

## 'LYBL' IN ACTION

### People Around You Reflect You

Take a moment to reflect on what people have said about you in the past in terms of what you "should be when you grow up".

Were they right?

Did you do what others thought you would?

Do any of their comments still resonate with you as something you'd like to pursue?

Was there a theme in underlying essence to all the suggestion?

Remember the label or package on what other people envisioned you doing (teacher, lawyer, artist) might not be the exact clue you're supposed to pick up.

Dissecting the essence of those labels makes all the difference.

# KEEP HOLD OF YOUR 'LYBL' JOURNAL!

## It's time to continue with your 'LYBL' in Action!

### 'LYBL' IN ACTION

#### Your Own Heroes Journey

If your purpose has not jumped off these pages into your consciousness yet, take this challenge.

Don't ask questions – just do it!
1. Talk to three to five people who know you well, personally or professionally or both
2. Ask them who they see you being to others and how they see you making a difference to people
3. Listen. Do not interrupt. Say "Thank You"

Now, do not question what they see.

That is only your mind trying to get in the way.

Write down their observations in your LYBL Journal and consider them in exploration.

# STILL KEEP HOLD OF YOUR 'LYBL' JOURNAL!

# WE ARE NOT DONE YET!

## It's time to continue with some more 'LYBL' in Action!

### 'LYBL' IN ACTION

#### Purpose Into Action

Use your LYBL Journal to creatively explore how you can put your lucrative purpose into action immediately.

Without expecting an immediate outcome, write down five to ten specifics you can do to put your purpose into action.

For example, once Rachel found her lucrative purpose, she resolved to put it into action by paying more attention to people than sales figures and by working on having more patience with everyone she came into contact with.

To guide you to find these specifics, consider the following questions:

- How will you spend your time differently to express your purpose on both career and personal life?
- How will you behave differently with the people in your life?
- What must change today for you to live your lucrative purpose?

Take your specific action steps and start living your purpose now.

# COACHES WRAP UP

Discovering your lucrative purpose is vital to the Action part of the process of connecting with your life blueprint, the one that is yours and yours alone.

To uncover and stay in touch with your lucrative purpose, you'll want to remember the following:

- Ask yourself: How do people utilise me? What do people come to me for? Then do more of whatever it is
- Dissect your dreams until you get to the essence of them. Put that essence into action right away
- Listen to the messages about yourself that people are trying to get you to hear, and act on them
- Go on your own heroes journey
- Live your purpose immediately by taking action, and observe how your life changes

# CHAPTER 7

# UNLEASH YOUR MAGNETIC
# SUPER POWERS

According to the dictionary, a magnet is something that attracts.

In this chapter, we will work on how to magnetise the field you inhabit so that you can attract 'good' people, accomplishments, opportunities and experiences into your life.

In the last chapter, we began to take the emphasis off of what you do and redirect it toward who you are.

We began to look beyond your job or life description on paper to uncover your true lucrative purpose.

As we saw, this purpose involves more than the dollars and cents in your life. It points you towards the most satisfying ways you can contribute to your world, whether in the context of raising your family or building a successful company.

In fact, attracting the work and purpose that leads you to your best life is the first step towards becoming a magnet.

Although we are still talking about the Action - that which we have to do to live our best life - after this chapter, we are crossing over into the 'Your Being' part of the equation.

Here, our Action will revolve around what you have to do to be who you need to be.

If you are confused by this, you won't be for long.

I will walk you through it in this chapter.

The elements that make up your life - the people, your circumstances, your achievements, your own sense of 'lucky' breaks and so on - can be termed the 'what' of your life.

Improving the quality of who we are starts to bring into our lives a higher quality of what.

For instance, becoming someone who has more confidence could aid you in finding the perfect job instead of jumping at the first opportunity. You will have to take action to become more confident, but it is this action that will get you results and could become more important than conventional goal setting and follow through.

What I am about to share with you is called the power of attraction.

The power of attraction challenges conventional wisdom, which says that positive results can occur only through linear and logical action and instead takes nonlinear approach.

It asks you to work on yourself from the inside out to bring about the outcomes you want.

Already, by making a personal manifesto and putting the focus of your activities on your lucrative purpose, you have begun this process already.

Here we will take it further, excavating your life blueprint even more.

The power of attraction means that you will attract what you want to you, spending less time chasing your desires and success.

# THE ENERGY EQUATION: FINDING YOUR BALANCE

The secret to attraction is to watch the energy equation in your life.

The energy equation is based on the concept that everything you do either gives you energy or robs you of energy.

Talking to some people may give you energy, talking to certain others might drain you. The way you deal with your financial life might enhance your life and energy, or it may be so consuming that it leaves you exhausted, with nothing to show for it.

Your frame of mind about an issue could help you move forward or it could drain you of the energy you need to tackle the problems.

In my experience, you are either moving toward what it is you are desiring or moving away.

Becoming a magnet for your best life means your magnet (you) needs to be positively charged in order to attract.

You must be engaged in relationships and activities that give you energy for your ability to attract to stay high.

If not, your magnet (you) will repel.

As you make yourself a magnet, you will monitor whether you are attracting or repelling in everything you do.

# IT'S TIME TO GRAB YOUR 'LYBL' JOURNAL!

The following box will assist you to distinguish the attitudes and behaviour of attraction from those of repulsion.

| 'LYBL' IN ACTION | |
|---|---|
| **How Are You As A Magnet?** | |
| *Characteristics that attract* | *Characteristics that repel* |
| Honouring your worth and time | Not honouring your worth and time |
| Expecting the best to happen | Worrying that the worst will happen |
| Doing your best | Cutting corners |
| Wanting everyone to succeed | Competing and wanting others to lose |
| Coming from your heart | Getting into power struggles |
| Maintaining integrity | Compromising values and ideals |
| Being aware and paying attention | Functioning on autopilot |

| Believing in abundance | Focusing on lack |
|---|---|
| Following your true desires | Forcing yourself to have to follow "have-to's" |
| Expressing gratitude and thanks | Feeling the world owes you |
| Enjoying the process and the journey | Valuing on the result or the goal |
| Making clear agreements | Having unspoken or vague expectations |
| Having clear intent and directed will | Having vague or undefined goals |
| Celebrating how far you've come | Focusing on how far you have to go |

Whenever you allow something like one of the items in the 'repel' column to impede the power of your magnet, your attention will be diverted from the good that waits you.

By taking care of everything that causes your magnet to repel, even if it's your own attitude, you create the opportunity for results to occur with less effort.

Your power to attract is minimised by any chaos in your life, so it must go.

That is why you made your personal manifesto.

You are meant to have this magnetic ability, just as you are meant to be wired for wisdom.

This is innate, but no-one gave you a manual on how to use it, so you are learning it now.

If you are attracting great opportunities, you'll know it.

Keep in mind that when things are going smoothly, energy is flowing; when things are bumpier, energy is spent in unproductive ways.

When you notice this happening in your life, you'll know this is the time to stop what you're doing and investigate.

Work out what needs to be cleared up to allow the energy to flow again.

The greater the energy flow, the higher your power to attract, and the clearer your life blueprint.

Your energy may be stuck for a variety of reasons – for instance, because you are struggling with something instead of getting help, because you have been hiding the truth about something (even from yourself!), or because you still have some Awakening to do with your own mind.

A friend once handed me a Chinese finger trap, a woven bamboo cylinder about the size of a $2 coin roll, asking that I insert my index fingers into either end. She then asked me to try and get my fingers out. My natural instinct was to pull hard from both ends. The cylinder tightened around my fingers. After many tries, it was clear that the only way out of the cylinder was to relax both fingers into it and gently ease each finger out.

The energy equation is similar.

If something is stuck, the harder you fight it, the harder it is to 'unstick' it, to solve it.

You waste your energy by resisting or fighting, and you gain energy by conserving it for the action that will make a difference.

The less you resist the problem, the easier it is to invite a solution.

# RAISE THE MAGNETIC VIBRATION IN YOUR LIFE

Let's focus now on four specific things you can do to increase the attraction quotient of your magnetism.

Each embodies elements from the magnetic chart on page 244, but they also include some new insights into what will make your magnet more attractive.

And as I draw your attention to it, you'll notice they all focus on who you have to be.

**Be a model of excellence**

Strive to benefit from the ease of attraction and demonstrate ideals that other people wish to emulate.

By being someone who people want to model part or themselves after, you'll find people drawn to you.

This puts you in the position of meeting up with more opportunities.

Being a model requires you and your life to be in great shape.

By now, I trust, we've put you on that path via your personal manifesto.

## Demonstrate certainty & ease

It gives people great comfort and certainty to be in the presence of someone who is even tempered and who seems to be sailing through life.

It also inspires them.

The energy is flowing evenly and attraction can occur.

Demonstrate ease with yourself, and positive magnetism will flow your way.

## Respect yourself

Treat yourself with a level of respect so that others will not dare to trespass upon you or your territory.

In addition, respecting yourself makes you attractive to others and raises your magnet's conductivity.

People want to be in the positive aura of a person who is confident in and of themselves.

**Invest time into others**

People don't care how much you know until they know how much you care.

As long as you're not overextending yourself, putting other people ahead of your own agenda is hugely effective in creating positive energy in your life.

As I've said before, people are the vehicle by which success will come to you, so it does make sense to invest in others.

You will see that your attraction factor will go up as you do so.

# IT'S TIME TO GRAB YOUR 'LYBL' JOURNAL!

## 'LYBL' IN ACTION

### What Is Your Attraction Factor?

$T$ake this quick quiz to test your attraction factor.

It examines the four methods to increase your positive conductivity, measuring which ones need improvement and attention on your way to attracting your best life.

Put a tick or a cross next to each item that accurately reflects how you are living right now.

| Be A Model Of Excellence | Tick or Cross |
|---|---|
| I set and live up to standards I truly want | |
| I do not promise more than I can deliver | |
| I put my integrity above all else | |

| | |
|---|---|
| I have more than enough of everything I need to live well | |
| I accept the bad with the good about myself | |
| I have extensive boundaries that keep other people's problems at bay | |
| **Demonstrate Certainty & Ease** | |
| I do not suffer or struggle | |
| I don't complain | |
| I ask plainly for what I need | |
| I don't react to problems | |
| I am solution oriented | |
| I am grateful for what I have, regardless of whether it is enough | |
| **Respect Yourself** | |
| I do not make excuses | |
| I admit when I am wrong | |
| I have a strong circle of friends who support me | |
| I am motivated internally, not externally | |
| I invest in myself and my growth | |
| I am in all my relationships by choice, not by obligation | |
| I take responsibility for all my problems and concerns | |
| **Invest Time Into Others** | |
| I put people ahead of results | |
| I don't just tell people I care – I show it | |
| I give people the credit and acknowledgement they deserve | |
| I can see faults in people and be compassionate and patient | |
| I am more interested in what others have to say than in being the centre of attention | |
| I speak to them in a way that makes them feel good about themselves, by highlighting what they do well | |

Count the number of ticks you made.

Your total is your attraction factor.

Here's what your score means.

**0-6:** Thanks for being honest. You're probably low on energy and have more than your share of challenges and problems. Now you know what to work on.

**7-13:** Your magnet is repelling quite a bit. Life could be easier, but you may now see what you need to do.

**14-20:** Good for you. Your magnet is attracting. You're probably feeling good and that is reflecting in your environment.

**21-25:** Congratulations! You're a magnet for the people and conditions you want in your life. Keep up the good work.

**D**id some of the items from the quiz jolt you a bit?

Is the entire notion of their being something to aspire to a foreign concept for you?

If so, you are experiencing the shifts that occur when you start framing your world from a whole different set of criteria than before.

If you are or were very externally referenced, measuring your happiness and success by others' approval and your material desires only, you will feel a little disorientated as you become internally referenced and start focusing on who you are being as a way to improve your life.

And that's all good ☺

If your score was not as yet where you desire it to be and would like to focus on changing it, study the rest of this chapter extremely carefully.

It will help you to attain more conductivity.

After you've digested the material and put it into effect, you may want to take the 'Attraction Factor' quiz again and see how your score has been influenced and changed.

# REDUCE YOUR SENSE OF SELF IMPORTANCE

Most of our energy goes to upholding our own importance.

It is our ego that upholds our importance and will often get in the way of attracting our best life.

It is therefore essential to the conductivity of our magnet that we reduce our ego and its importance.

I have heard it said that the work of a coach can be likened to 'ego reduction therapy.' An effective coach knows to keep in check their own ego's need to have the answers and be right, in order to tap into the wisdom and answers their client already has.

When you decide to reduce your ego (the part of you that is full of fight and always wanting to feel justified and be right), you begin to expand yourself, your wisdom and the memory of your soul – who you are in essence.

The goal here is to bring these inner qualities to your outer material world and refrain from constantly trying to message your ego with affirmations of how important you are.

If you can do this, you will produce changes in your life in a gentler, more low-impact way.

Granted, if your job puts you in the middle of a dog-eat-dog world and you want to stay firmly in that field, reducing your importance will be a very difficult thing to do.

However, ego reduction helps bring about results in an unconventional way.

It may take a little longer to get results, but trust me, your investment in the process will be worth it.

You already have the innate ability to attract results this way, if only your self-importance would let you believe that was enough.

One of my first experiences with ego reduction will illustrate how this concept can be surprisingly effective in increasing your power to attract.

As soon as I gave up nursing for good, an invitation arrived for a party given by the University Student Association associated with my intake year. I decided to go, wearing the first business suit I'd ever bought, which I thought of as my 'I am in business now' costume.

Since I had never been to an event like this before, I was nervous about how I should behave and what I should say. I was not yet used to my new identity of 'businesswoman' and scared of networking, so I decided to use the magnet theory.

I would say nothing, avoid schmoozing, and see if I could attract people to me by being a magnet.

Once I was at the party, although my mind and ego were screaming that I should do something. I stood in the middle of the room and made eye contact only with whomever I wanted to.

At different times, several people stopped by to ask who I was and what I did. By the end of the evening I had business cards from three potential clients, I remember one of them in particular, a woman who said, "There's something about your energy, I don't know, but I was drawn to talk to you".

Our need to uphold our importance forces us to feel as if we have to impress or take action in order to have an impact.

I trust my example assists you to see how who we are can itself be enough.

# IT'S TIME TO GRAB YOUR 'LYBL' JOURNAL!

## 'LYBL' IN ACTION

### Reducing Your Sense Of Self Importance

Return to the "What Is Your Attraction Factor" quiz and choose an item from the "Demonstrate Certainty & Ease" or "Invest Time Into Others" section that would assist you to reduce your own sense of self importance / ego.

Put the item into action for the next twenty-four hours, and record your impressions in your LYBL Journal.

For example, if you choose "I am more interested in what others have to say than being the centre of attention", from the "Invest Time Into Others" section, you could spend the next 24 hours being a much more attentive listener – asking more questions and being curious – and then record in your journal what that did to your ego and how you felt.

Was it hard?

Did you have to struggle to pay attention?

What was the benefit?

What about this experience is worth repeating and making a part of who you are?

# YOUR ENERGY EXCHANGES AND VIBRATIONAL FREQUENCY

It's one thing to sit in a room and imagine attracting results or to do as I did at that cocktail party; however, these aren't the activities we normally fill our days with.

The way we apply this to everyday life is to keep an eye on the energy exchanges in your life.

Energy exchanges occur in many ways: between you and other people, between you and your money, between you and your career.

Granted, these criteria for judging your day and activities will probably be quite different from what you are used to, but measuring your success in energy can assist you to understand why you may not be living the life you want.

As we said earlier, everything you have and do will either give you energy or rob it from you.

The energy will either get stuck or flow.

When it's stuck, we experience frustration; when it flows, we flourish.

When we are stuck and our energy is being drained, our conductivity or vibration (the ability to attract) is low and we are not at our best.

When the energy flows, our best self can reign, our conductivity is high and we can be a magnet.

To monitor the energy exchanges in your life, detect the places where you need to stop doing so much and start making adjustments to who you are being.

In other words, you have to observe how you are acting in the situation. This strategy, however, will work best when you have taken responsibility for your life and taken actions as we discussed in implementing your personal manifesto in Chapter 5.

# 'LYBL' STORY: ENTER KELLY AND JAMES

A client named Kelly was always nervous about her finances, despite the fact that she was doing all the 'right' things – saving while paying down her debt, following a budget, investing wisely, and so on.

Nevertheless, she never felt financially secure, no matter how much money she was making or how well her investments were doing. Her lack of comfort with her finances was a huge energy drain in her life.

Kelly compared her situation with her friend James, who had been in the same boat financially when they met.

Over the years, James had made a lot of money, saved wisely and led a prosperous lifestyle, even though he hardly cared at all about the specifics of his financial condition, such as the yield on his investments. Kelly was frustrated that her efforts to manage her money did not pay off in the same way things had for James.

It was clear to me that my client was taking the same responsible actions as her friend, so I asked Kelly one day, "What does James do that you don't?"

"He doesn't worry, complain or constantly obsess about it" she answered.

That was exactly the point.

Kelly used some of the suggestions in Chapter 3 to gain perspective and her magnet's conductivity and vibration increased.

Within six months she reported feeling 'richer'.

The numbers reflected that, as well as her state of mind.

So, who do you have to be and what do you need to change in order to have an even energy exchange with...your money? Your family? Your friends? Your work colleagues? Your life?

Can you distinguish between what consumes your life's energy and what enhances it?

The dead give away is your energy level.

What is increasing it and what is robbing energy from you?

# IT'S TIME TO GRAB YOUR 'LYBL' JOURNAL!

## 'LYBL' IN ACTION

### 12 Hour Energy Watch

Go on an energy watch for 12 waking hours.

During this time, pay very close attention to every activity and person you encounter and monitor your energy level.

Did the task, conversation or meal you ate add to your level of energy or take from it?

When you spoke with certain people, did you feel energised or drained?

Where applicable, who were you being in these situations?

Were you part of the problem or the solution?

Were you draining your own energy with your attitude or anxiety, or were you drained by the other person or by what they were doing?

Capture each thing you notice and record it into your LYBL Journal, and see where the energy 'vampires' are in your life.

These could be other people, certain activities, or even yourself – that is, your own choices about where to invest your energy or the way in which you might let other people or situations affect you.

Also, please keep in mind that adrenaline, coffee, sugar, energy drinks or any other rush-producing substance does not count as an energy enhancer.

The energy boost these things provide is not sustainable; therefore it ends up being more of an energy drain than an energy enhancer.

# 'LYBL' STORY: MEET ANGELA

### ENERGY EXCHANGE BALANCE IS CRITICAL

Angela, a mother of two and a part-time insurance broker, had come to coaching to get the most out of her business.

As we worked on her business strategies, we also examined the rest of her life.

For instance, Angela complained about always feeling tired and she had frequent colds and sinus infections.

Angela's mother, who called her about three times a day, claimed to not be able to make a decision without her daughter's assistance.

Ever since she was widowed, she had relied heavily on Angela. Angela felt taking care of her mother was her duty.

When Angela did the energy watch coaching exercise, much to her dismay, her mother came up as one of the biggest energy drains in her life.

Although this was hard to acknowledge, it was undeniable that her mother's dependence, as well as her hypercritical nature, had become a very heavy burden.

In making this discovery, it became clear to Angela why she always felt worn out.

Nonetheless, Angela was terrified as the thought of having to correct the situation. Like most people would, she thought any possible way to do so would devastate her mother. Then she was laid up for three weeks with the flu. Lying in bed with barely enough energy to lift her head, she worked out in her mind what she could tell her mother to correct the energy exchange between them and increase her own positive magnetism.

As her mother telephoned with her daily appeals for help and direction, Angela began responding by saying things like, "What do you think Mum?", "What are you going to do, Mum?" and

"I know you've been used to me doing everything for you, but I am going to be a little more selfish with my time these days, so I hope you'll also ask your other kids to help you too."

These were difficult things for Angela to say, but she was patient and persistent and she held her resolve when her mother felt threatened or lost her temper.

Once her mother got over the initial shock of the rules changing, there was a huge, positive difference in their relationship. It became a more loving one, and Angela stopped resenting her mother and was much more helpful in kinder, more profound ways.

She felt more energised by their exchanges and over time, had fewer colds and sinus problems.

Her business also increased by twenty per cent, because she had more time and energy to focus on what mattered there.

By correcting this energy exchange with her mother, this daughter even increased her income.

## WATCH YOUR OFF THE RICHTER MAGNETISM

By watching the energy exchanges in your life, you are managing the quality of your life and have gone on a level deeper in excavating your life blueprint.

You attract results instead of chasing them.

As you become more and more 'attractive', you'll have to watch out for the one danger in all this.

The fact is you can be too attractive and too magnetic if you don't know how to control the magnetism.

When you are attracting people at an astounding rate, there may be more people and opportunities than you can reasonably take advantage of without exhausting yourself.

When you become a viable magnet, other people can't even articulate why they want to be in your company – they are just drawn to you.

All this attention can be too much for anyone.

It is too easy to fall prey to wanting to meet all the needs of these outside influences.

What to do – or should I say, who to be?

Be someone who is clear on what their criteria is for what they will allow into their life. As harsh as it may sound, it will become essential for you to continually monitor the quality of who and what comes into your life.

As you excavate the 'higher-quality' you, you'll have to become clearer and clearer about who and what keeps your energy high.

You may find that some of the aspects of your life that were okay before have begun to drain you.

Therefore, you'll need criteria for your life.

As you attract more and more people and opportunities, you'll need some measure to weed through it all.

The next section will guide you.

# KNOW YOUR OWN KRYPTONITE AND MAKE PEACE WITH IT

If you are still adjusting to the idea of looking at your life in terms of energy and magnetism, it might help to realise that the common denominator is recognising what is and what is not acceptable to you in your life.

Our work is leading you towards the recognition, so that problems can be kept to a minimum and your conductivity can be restored and enhanced.

As you decide more and more quickly what can stay in your life and what must go, you will get better at learning to say "no".

You will be able to distinguish between attracting gold and attracting lint, and you will communicate it in a way that keeps your energy level high without lowering the energy of anyone around you.

Being able to identify what is acceptable to you and what is not can sound trivial, but most of us allow so much more to happen to us and around us than we have to.

This can take the form of the 'deer in headlights' effect, where you don't even know you were hurt until after it's over. I also call it getting slimed (as in Ghostbusters), someone does something completely inappropriate to you (for instance, raising her voice, making a rude remark, acting in a threatening manner) and you just stand there taking it, in stunned perplexity.

For a person, action, remark or event to be unacceptable, it doesn't even have to be blatantly wrong. It could just be something that does not fit with what you want for your life or that makes you uncomfortable.

What it does do is take energy from you and lower your magnet's ability to attract, by taking time, energy and attention away from what matters to you.

For example, it may be unacceptable that your neighbours are cold and unresponsive. You could be cold right back, or you could extend yourself to them in an effort to get to know them. Imagining that after several attempts to get closer to your neighbours, the situation remains unchanged. Knowing that you tried and letting it go may be exactly what it takes to make the situation okay again for you.

Making something acceptable does not necessarily mean you have to fix or solve it; sometimes, you merely have to make peace with it.

Reconciling something like this for yourself allows the energy to flow again, which allows your magnetism to increase its intensity.

In order to do that, you are asking yourself to stretch how you are being in the situation.

You have to decide who you want to be about this instance versus what you want to do.

The result is peace of mind and permission to return to your best life.

# 'LYBL' STORY: ENTER WAYNE

### FIND YOUR MAGNETIC VOICE

Wayne was a designer at a desktop publishing firm who came to me for coaching.

He was an efficient worker, often getting his assignments done early.

Whenever that happened, he would create some of his own graphic designs on the job. No one seemed to mind – in fact, his extra work inspired a lot of people who shared his office.

One woman Clare frequently stopped at his desk to see what he was working on. In the most innocent way, she would ask if she could use one of his ideas or base a project of hers on something she'd see him do. He couldn't think of a good enough reason to say "no", so he let her.

As Wayne and I were discussing how he could become a magnet for opportunity and some of the areas of his life that were acceptable and unacceptable, his work environment came up for exploration.

All of a sudden, Wayne started getting angry.

He could barely contain himself as he shouted: "It is completely unacceptable to me that my work colleagues use my ideas!"

He'd been bottling up these feelings for so long that it felt great to voice them out loud.

Wayne realised that he was annoyed because of both his protective feelings towards his own work and his frustration with Clare for not recognising her own ample talents.

As we looked at ways to communicate his feelings to Clare, he decided that he would no longer give her his work; instead, he would encourage her to come up with her own ideas and offer some assistance.

This is how he phrased it: "Clare, it's unacceptable to me that you don't see that you can come up with good ideas too. It's not okay for you to look at my work anymore. Let me know how else I can assist you to come up with some of your own".

Giving everything doesn't make you a magnet – it simply leaves you drained.

On the other hand, when you give out information about your boundaries and what you are willing to do, your magnetism is left intact and can even help others much more than you may think.

Wayne set a very clear boundary about what actions were and were not permitted, thus making his position known to Clare without hurting her.

Although at first she didn't appreciate the challenge, once she came up with some great ideas of her own, she saw how his policy was ultimately better for her.

This most productive way to say no is not to tear the other person down, but to work to build them up.

Doing this will increase your magnetism.

# IT'S TIME TO GRAB YOUR 'LYBL' JOURNAL!

## 'LYBL' IN ACTION

### Saying "NO"

The next time you have to say "no" to something you had once thought acceptable, follow these steps to do so in a productive way:

1. Determine what is unacceptable
2. Take responsibility, for what is unacceptable; don't make it the other party's fault
3. State specifically what is not okay with you
4. Ask for the change(s), you'd like to see
5. When appropriate, offer support in a new way

# HOW WOULD YOU LIKE IT TO BE?

So far in this chapter, we've explored the conditions that repel and attract, the impact of energy exchanges in your life and how the unacceptable can be an obstacle to your ultimate conductivity.

It's now time to examine what will fuel your magnetic ability the most: identifying the ideal for every part of your life.

When you explore what is ideal, what you really want, you can accelerate the rate at which you attract results.

The ideal is the best-case scenario, the dream, the wish, the best circumstances you can imagine.

The ideal is an inspiring vision and direction motivated from within.

Your ideal doesn't have to be heady or grandiose either.

It can be used in everyday, practical terms. For example, what is your ideal work schedule, who is your ideal baby sitter, what is your ideal job description, or who is your ideal lawyer or bookkeeper?

Notice I did not use the word 'perfect', which is not the same thing as 'ideal'.

Perfection tends to be rigid.

When we look for the ideal, we may have perfection as a goal but we retain enough flexibility to find something different, perhaps even better, that we may not have anticipated.

In my opinion, being a perfectionist is the ultimate lack of self-acceptance, in that we need the outside world to reflect perfection so that we can know we are okay.

That is why perfectionism can be so rigid and so damaging and why the search for perfection will repel instead of attract.

The ideal attracts because it's meant to be a receptacle to contain your dream.

Think of it like a pitcher holding water.

If we don't allow the water to be kept in a container, it could run off, dry up, disperse or evaporate.

Similarly, without something to catch them, our dreams for ourselves can disappear or we can lose track of them.

When you hold the vision of an ideal scenario for some part of your life, you have created criteria by which to measure your present circumstances and those that show up as your work towards living your best life.

Sometimes we have an ideal situation in mind and we will surpass that ideal.

Other times, what we thought was ideal is not so when we attain it.

Regardless, having the picture allows you to follow your own wisdom.

# IT'S TIME TO GRAB YOUR 'LYBL' JOURNAL!

## 'LYBL' IN ACTION

### Your Ideal Scenario

For each area of your life (relationships, career/work, money, health, well-being, physical environment etc.) or anything else you are looking to improve or create.

1. Write down and describe what the ideal scenario looks like. If you could have what you truly wanted for this part of your life, what would it be? Be specific, and resist the temptation to edit yourself. For example, if your ideal career is in an organisation with people you look forward to seeing every morning, where you are able to double your current salary and you have to only do the part of the job that you love – say, talking to clients – then write that down

2. Write down and describe what's real and true about this part of your life now. What is missing? What are your complaints?

3. If you are not yet living your ideal scenario, write down five steps (or as many as you need) that could connect the real with the ideal. (Use the highlighted action points from the 'LYBL' Through Writing exercise titled, 'You Already Know What Needs To Be Done' on pages to guide you.)

4. Once you've written the ideal scenario for as many parts of your life as you would like to improve, you must take action. Only action can make it real. Get the support you need to keep you accountable, prod you along, and help you or to simply cheer you on. And remember, use your written ideal scenario as a measuring stick for what you allow in your life. It's okay to say no to some person or situation that does not fit the ideal. It takes courage to be able to trust that by saying "no" you are leaving room for the "yes" (the ideal) to come along.

# NAME IT, WRITE IT, SPEAK IT, CLAIM IT – OWN IT!

In this part of the book, you are letting who you really are shine through, and as you've improved your life's infrastructure by delivering on your personal manifesto, you are ready for bigger things.

That is why we are spending time on 'the ideal'.

You may find that the desires and actions you described in the 'LYBL Through Writing' coaching exercise above were more radical or have assisted you to expect more for yourself than anything you wrote in your personal manifesto.

Earlier, we had to let our life tell us what it needed from us.

Once we have done that and made the foundation solid, we can turn the tables once again, and start asking more from our life and ourselves.

Not in the painful ways in which we might have done before we read this far, but in a way that does not allow us to lose.

By the time you reach this stage of excavating your blue print, your life should be in good enough shape that even if you do not reach the ideal, you've lost nothing and gained everything.

When the consolation prize is already pretty terrific, going for the ideal becomes a painless gamble.

And ironically, when we can have that freedom to pursue the ideal with ease and detachment, it is more likely that we can achieve it.

That said, the final key to attracting the ideal is being specific.

As you saw in one of the items from the chart on pages called "How Are You As A Magnet?" being specific is important to your ability to attract.

Furthermore, being specific even if what you want seems out of your league may be just the energy your magnet needs to bring the 'improbable' thing to you.

When you can name it, you can claim it, when you can speak it, it can be yours.

The next story illustrates what I mean.

# 'LYBL' STORY: MEET CHRISSIE

## SPECIFICITY WILL DELIVER YOUR IDEAL

Once her son turned two, Chrissie wanted to return to work and set about finding the most appropriate day-care situation.

After checking out the best nurseries in the area, she was very frustrated and unhappy with what was available.

She wondered if she was being too picky as the start date for her job loomed.

I asked Chrissie to write a profile of her ideal day-care provider.

As she listed the situation she wanted for her son and the kind of activities and people she wanted him to be with, she realised she had been barking up the wrong tree.

She had thought a nursery was the best choice she could make as a parent and yet the ideal profile she had written more accurately described a home-care situation.

Chrissie was afraid she could not afford this pricier option, so I asked her to include the ideal price in her profile.

During the next two weeks, Chrissie kept her written profile with her, asked her friends, put an ad in the paper and was overwhelmed with the responses.

She soon found someone who fit most, if not all, of the criteria, including the price.

The ideal profile had helped her attract what she wanted very quickly.

Its clearness and specificity had been important elements in experiencing attraction and becoming a magnet.

Any problem you're confronted with is also an opportunity to grow, to choose wisely and to do your best.

It is a chance to gain new skills that will become a permanent part of who you are.

It is how we grow through these situations that determine our wisdom.

If we face the lesson and grow through it, we are wiser.

If we resist, avoid or otherwise delay our growth, we keep the wisdom at bay.

We choose to lead a more difficult life.

One of my mentors always says, "As magnets, we attract who and what we are ready for; the only way to attract better is to grow, grow, grow."

# COACHES WRAP UP

**A**s we leave the Action portion of this book, you have the tools and insights you need to be responsible for your life and start enjoying the benefits of the journey you've undertaken. Making yourself a super magnet with super magnetic powers will be invaluable as you move from the work of the doing to reaping the rewards of your best life.

As you work on living your best life, a fulfilling one that is not a struggle to sustain, remember these points to raise the conductivity of your magnetic forces:

- Concentrate on who you are being, not what you are doing
- Raise your magnetic forces and vibration by being a model of excellence, demonstrating certainty and ease, respect yourself and investing time into others
- Watch the way in which you exchange your energy
- Know what is unacceptable for you and communicate boundaries
- Dream big and deal with the ideal
- Be specific
- Take action and grow, grow, grow!

# PART THREE

# YOUR BEING

*"Our whole spiritual transformation brings us to the point where we realise that in our own being, we are enough."*

—Ram Dass

As you progress through the three stages of excavating your life's blueprint, your degree of consciousness will increase, although you may not be aware of it. By now you should have evidence that your wisdom wiring is reliable and intact.

That you, and your wisdom, are now starting to hum along together quite nicely.

Your new level of awareness is what will allow things to happen more quickly. You will not need as much energy, nor will it take so much effort to manage your life or to make new things happen. You will be making different choices, which will require less repetition of old patterns that used to cause you pain. You won't have to repeat the same mistakes over and over before you 'learn your lesson'. In fact, it will seem as if you won't have as many hard lessons to learn.

All this allows good things to happen in your life more quickly.

In your new state of being, you'll find that it doesn't take as much knowledge to feel secure and move forward in your life. Your knowledge is there. Your wisdom is there. You can feel confident about this. If you don't feel this then go back and review your weak points in the strategies we've covered so far.

In the stage of 'Your Being', you will start to trust yourself more and you'll be able to take action based solely on what you feel is right. You'll have stopped relying solely on doing as the only confirmation of your worth and existence, so you'll be free to move through life with more ease, being more comfortable with who you are.

In this section, you are going to let go.

You have finished the self-exploration that comes with awakening and the rethinking, exploring and fixing that comes through your actions.

You've taken action in so many parts of your life. Now finally we are going into free fall – 'Your Being'.

Be prepared to feel lighter, and in fact, it is here that I would like to acknowledge a beautiful woman on this earth, one of my coaches, mentors and soul sisters, Rachel Anastasi for her metaphor of popping corn.

For it is here, in 'Your Being' that you have journeyed from 'Your Awakening' as a tightly packed corn kernel, had the heat turned up as you confronted 'Your Actions', before arriving here at 'Your Being' as a popped, light, fluffy, expanded piece of popcorn.

Remember, we are human beings, not humans doing.

It is essential to become comfortable with being.

The place where you relinquish effort and control and still expect a great outcome.

Without this 'Your Being' section, you would not be complete and I would not have done my job of achieving my desired outcome for you.

Here, we will tap into the resources of the spirit to put the final touches on your excavation of your life blueprint.

For the purpose of this section, let's define spirituality as the belief that there is some kind of unspoken universal connection among all humankind. The specifics of that belief – whether in God, angels, spirit guides, a universal force, the self (and only the self), or some other type of entity – doesn't matter.

All that matters is that you are willing to explore tapping into that collective consciousness for your own benefit and that of others – that you consider there is a reserve of untapped information out there that can facilitate the unfolding of the life you are meant to live.

It does not matter what your religious persuasion is – or even if you have one – because I will not interfere with the principles and philosophies of your belief system.

I will however, ask you to stretch beyond your comfort zone to explore new parts of yourself. In fact, I may not even ask this of you, by now, we are like family, and you will know that this goes with the program, so I will be able to demand this of you, because you will want nothing less than to demand this of yourself.

Without veering too far from the practical approach we have taken so far, we will delve into three areas that encourage you to trust your life is on autopilot toward the best version of itself.

That your co-ordinates are well on track for you to travel safe and well.

Mastering silence, harnessing your intuition and giving up the need to know are the tools needed to draft the final pieces of your blue print.

In my opinion, this is the most fun, and essential part for your life's blueprint to take flight.

# CHAPTER 8

# BECOME A MASTER OF
# FOCUS & BEING

Mastering focus may sound like an action-oriented process, yet nothing could be further from the truth. Mastering focus depends on becoming still, something that usually defies most conventional wisdom on how to get what you want from life.

Because to get what you want out of life, you must always be taking action... right? Wrong! And if you thought 'yes', you will need to go all the way back to the start of this book to understand why, and as you do you will embrace that this is all part of your own personal journey to get you to where you need to go.

Nothing is a better partner to taking action than being still. Stillness allows the most effective action to emerge, allowing us to settle the chaos and uncover the action and direction that will do most good.

You might wonder why this book did not start with this section, since it reveals the most wisdom in our lives (and yes, Benjamin Reeves that thought was inspired by you!).

Quite simply, you would not have been ready for this. The work we have done up to now has cleared the way to being able to master focus and being.

In this chapter, we will explore three ways of mastering focus and learning how to be.

1. Focus and being through silence
2. Focus and being through intention
3. Focus and being on your own life, not on the lives of others

These three elements deliver huge force when it comes to having an impact on the quality of your life. Once the other pieces we have described in the previous strategies are in place, these elements of focus can be really effective in creating results with seemingly little effort.

And that is what I believe living your best life is all about.

# TO FIND YOUR WAY: BE STILL

In our fast-paced, busy world, the last thing we may feel we have time for is finding a few moments of quiet in each day.

When I first recommend silence as a coaching exercise to my clients, some resist the idea or, at best, try to implement it with great skepticism.

Almost invariably and without any doubt, they soon discover the benefits to be found in making the time to be still.

Over time, several important things happen in silence. Your true values begin to emerge. Your own priorities come to the forefront and take precedence over those of the day's schedule and the world around you.

Any decision you come to in silence is based on strength and wisdom.

Practicing silence allows for clarity and order to emerge. Its cumulative effect adds up to less reliance on schedules and to-do lists and more understanding of the natural priority and order of things.

When you become comfortable with silence, you invite a natural organisation to your life that doesn't require much effort and control. Practicing silence also increases the power of your ability to do things that will make a real difference in your day. I call this my 'KAPOW' list. Many of my clients have reported that as they learned to be still, they would seem to get their work done more quickly and even find themselves with extra time to get ready for the next day.

Most of the time, the things we do require only one side (right or left) of our brain. Practicing silence yields a higher output of organisation, clarity and calm because it causes the two hemispheres of our brain to work together in unison.

The alpha state that this creates allows for the broader scope of awareness and the tapping into of our full potential. In this relaxed state lies the greatest and most beautiful pool of your innate wisdom. The more we go into this state the easier it is for the brain to produce this state on its own. That is why it gets easier with practice and why it has a cumulative effect.

Allow me to walk you through several ways to practice silence in this chapter so that you can access it with grace and ease at any time you should need to.

In order to effectively allow silence to be our natural organiser, we need to be comfortable with silence and be comfortable in it.

So often, silence makes us feel uncomfortable.

It does that, because it asks us to grow. We have to grow to accumulate what we face in that silent space. Most of us would rather have dental surgery than feel the discomfort of battling with ourselves. Silence allows the truth to be revealed. It allows you to willingly give up your illusions in favour of this truth. In silence, you will be able to hear and see the real you and the priorities that will best express you.

I have also witnessed this first hand, time and time again, noticing that people will often rush to fill a space or silence because of the level of discomfort they find there. When coaching clients, it is actually this silence where clients find what it is they need. Time and time again it has been proven to me that a vacuum of space must be created before any new thoughts can rush in to fill it. Embrace the silence, create the space and watch the magic appear.

Silence is that suspended moment when life holds its breath to allow you to catch yours.

Silence is the greatest form of intimacy.

The silences in a conversation are those places where the words stop and the souls can meet. We all long for these quiet places, we even crave them, but many of us are terrified to visit them. We keep talking. We forget to breathe. We fill our lives with endless activities to avoid touching the inner core that silence unveils.

You may have noticed that I haven't used the word 'meditation' here. Many people find that word intimidating. People feel they must know how to meditate before trying to embrace silence as a daily practice in their life.

However, although practicing silence is meditation, there is not one set way to do it. Before I had ever been formally taught any meditative techniques, I had succeeded for years at finding ways to quiet my mind.

I am about to share with you different ways that I have found to practice silence.

And of course, I know you will already have a few of your own to add.

There is only one requirement that I have; that you do find time to be quiet every day.

Practicing silence daily is necessary if you're going to learn to cultivate awareness and a higher state of mind that it can provide. How you choose to practice silence is up to you, as long as you achieve the goal of quiet contemplation, probably the one principle all spiritual and religious practices hold in common.

I often get asked how I maintain my energy levels and energetic approach to life. Hand on heart, I know that practicing silence and mindfulness has been the magic ingredient to remaining energetically vibrant.

Mastering silence can however come with its obstacles. You can expect both your mind and your body to fidget. Your mind will wander. If you are very new to the practice of sitting in silence, you may be tempted to give up immediately. Try to do as well as you can, keeping in mind that finding silence and being still does not need to be done perfectly. Soon you'll find your mind and body adjusting more readily to times in silence.

You may want to practice thinking of silence as plugging into an energy source. Imagine recharging your battery to your mobile phone. We all know that it's best to recharge it fully, but even if you can only charge it for a few minutes, the phone will run longer and last the distance.

Choosing the time to be silent is your first step. In the morning just after rising, and at night just before bed are often considered convenient times, because these times are already filled with daily rituals. Silence can easily become a new, valued ritual. Like an added bonus extra!

You may however, choose to be silent at some point during the day. Some people use their office; others find time for silence just before gearing up to do the biggest task of the day. If you are home with kids, it can be more challenging – however, some clients have found that inviting their children to join them allows them to avoid being distracted and models quiet time for their children. And what an awesome gift to pass down to your children.

When you find your time for your silence is your choice, but it will need to be a time that you can count on keeping with yourself. As you get used to how you feel when you've become silent, you'll find you can enter that centred and grounded place almost instantly anywhere you may be, whether waiting in a queue somewhere, sitting on the train, or even while enduring an endless meeting at the office. The more you practice, the more positive influences of silence can be yours anywhere.

The most important part of focusing on silence is knowing that facing yourself in the silence will generate more and more rewards in time.

# 'LYBL' STORY: ENTER ROB

## ALLOW SILENCE TO BE YOUR FRIEND

Rob had recently been promoted to a management position in a large international recruiting firm that specialised in recruitment management software. Feeling even more pressure to perform well, he hired me as his coach to help him become a better manager. In a five-week coaching crash course, we improved his communication style, his organisation and delegation skills and his ability to develop and build upon new and existing relationships.

Once his main concerns were taken care of and he had made the progress he was initially seeking, I knew we had to get stuck into the 'real' work that Rob had in front of him.

As I do with most clients, I asked Rob to start making room in his life for fifteen minutes of silence a day. When he found this incredibly difficult, we reduced the time to five minutes, but even that didn't work. We looked at what made spending five minutes in silence so hard for him, and found that while Rob had lived by himself for some time, he had developed habits to keep from ever really being alone with himself. He kept the TV or radio on as background noise; he smoked and drank wine in the evening. In summary, anything to avoid confronting himself or listening to himself in the silence.

Although Rob repeatedly asked to put giving up smoking in his personal manifesto, I would not let him. To my mind, such a specific 'giving up' goal would have been a distraction to the real work of learning to be still and discovering himself in the silence created. At my recommendation, Rob started changing his focus on the brisk walk he took with his dog every morning. Instead of looking at the homes and cars on their route, he began to take deeper breaths and to concentrate on the trees and the birds as he walked.

Soon, he was ready to sit still for three to five minutes daily. He learned to focus on his breathing and, after practicing some of the techniques you will learn in this chapter, he began to turn off his 100-kilometres-per-hour mind and dwell in the real mental quiet that his silent time made possible.

As summer arrived, Rob took a break from our coaching, enjoying time with family at the beach on weekends and working a slower week. When he came back in autumn, he announced with pride that he had given up smoking and drinking! I asked what had changed, and he replied, "One day, I just woke up and realised I was trying to kill myself with this stuff. I didn't need to do that anymore."

The silence had stepped in as his friend, and Rob got in touch with the part of himself who really did want to live fully, and he was then able to access his own sense of power in a new way.

I had known that the only way he would quit his unresourceful habits was by addressing them at this soul level. Until then he had been afraid to connect with himself. Once he did, he found the opening for so much more: his health, a sense of mental well-being, new interests, old passions and even a satisfying romantic relationship.

Allow silence to be your friend, because you simply never know what you will find there, for a lot of people they find everything they felt they had lost.

## WHERE TO FIND SILENCE

Now that I've told you what practicing silence can do for you, it's time to get down to the specifics of how you can reach this state.

**Find a Place and a Time that Suits You**

Find a comfortable place to take your silent time. You might create a special place in your home devoted to this activity. It could be a chair or a place where you are comfortable on the floor. You might want to sit on a pillow. Make sure you are comfortable, because it will interfere with your ability to focus if you are not. I encourage you though, NOT to lie down.

Okay, I know, I am already hearing you ask me, "If I am going to meditate first thing in the morning or last thing at night, why not do it lying down?" You're already in bed, right?

The reason is you are too likely to fall asleep and the brain activity of sleep is different to practicing silence.

You need to be conscious, yet in a suspended state of higher awareness. Lying down won't do. Neither will browsing through a magazine, checking Facebook, scrolling through your SMS's or relaxing with a book or newspaper. Silence means still and without any distractions.

My husband and I have now implemented no technology times into our daily lives to allow this to occur, and also to allow us to be more present with one another. I suggest you do too!

**Get Off Your Butt and Move**

If sitting still will never be your thing, then give walking a go as your silent activity. Get off your butt and take a brisk walk outside, it may be even more effective to pace a small area where you can pay close attention to what your body is doing. As you would if you were practicing tai chi, which is a discipline of motion, notice your weight and how it moves. Notice how you plant your feet and how your muscles move. Stay focused on the movement of your body as a way to remove the chatter from your mind.

I have found yoga to be the most wonderful practice for me in this regard, followed closely by swimming.

## Go Outside and Connect With Nature

I draw so much power and energy from nature. If you ever feel stifled from spending too much time indoors, find a spot outside where you can sit in peace and listen to nature humming all around you. When and where possible, remove your shoes so you can feel the earth, this will allow you to feel more grounded. Even within the sounds of nature you will hear silence.

## Candles & Incense

Lighting candles and incense often sets the appropriate mood for silence and intimacy. When you observe the flame, you will notice the focus it brings to your mind. Imagine the radiance of the candlelight reflecting the same radiance you have inside. At times, when I do this, I visualise and feel myself becoming the light.

Internal radiance is the result of a successful session of silence.

This is exactly why I created the luscious and luxurious range of LYBL candles, for people to enjoy in this way. You simply must check out my signature fragrance – Coconut Lime!

Lighting incense for me is a symbol and way of recognising silence in my own mind, allowing my thoughts to drift off with the fragrant smoke that it produces. Fragrant blend? Nag Champra of course.

## Breathe…Remember to Breathe

You may choose to focus on your breathing as a way to the silence. Follow your breath as it fills your lungs and is released through your nose or mouth. Observe it until your time is up or you have forgotten to do so because you are in a Zen-like state. Take ten deep breaths to start this working for you. Inhale slowly, and exhale even more slowly. Silently count to four as you inhale, and eight as you exhale. Increase the number, as you get better at it. Even if all you do is take these ten breaths before starting and ending your day, it will make a difference in your life. I have adopted many yogic breathing techniques into my day, that when used allow me to feel more balanced, more centred, more grounded.

## Feel Your Way to Silence

Stroke your cat or dog, feeling a beautiful fabric that's soft and inviting such as a beautiful plush blanket, the smoothness of silk under your fingers, a smooth stone that has been washed up on the beach or the suns rays as they absorb into you. Whatever your item of choice, feeling your way to silence is an ultimate form of focus. Use this technique and sense of touch as a way to relax, let go and stay in silence.

# IT'S TIME TO GRAB YOUR 'LYBL' JOURNAL!

## 'LYBL' IN ACTION

### Busy World to Silent World

Here are some things that will assist you to make the sometimes challenging transition from your busy world to your silent world.

- **Brain Dump:** Write down your distractions. Make your to-do list. Write down what you're worried about forgetting. Empty your mind onto a piece of paper. Then begin to find the silence. I call this 'Brain Dumping' because it invites you to dump all of the things that are occupying your mind into your notebook and release them. Free up the space and allow your wisdom to step in.
- **Inspirational Readings:** Keep a collection of poems, spiritual readings, inspirational quotes or

self-help literature close to the place where you have chosen to practice silence. Access these to start shifting gears and lowers speeds in your mind.

- **Gratitude:** Mentally listing what you are grateful for will help shift you into a space of silence readiness. You may even find to keep a regular record in your LYBL Journal of what you are grateful for helpful. You can refer to this at any time you feel like moving into your silent world.

- **Spiritual Prayer:** If you have a spiritual or religious prayer that you are accustomed to, this is a great way to begin being silent. I have even found chanting to be a beautiful way for me to start accessing my silent world.

# KEEP HOLD OF YOUR 'LYBL' JOURNAL!

## It's time to continue with your 'LYBL' Action!

### 'LYBL' IN ACTION

#### Be Silent

It's time to be silent. Aim for fifteen minutes of silence a day. Start with a shorter period if you need to, and do it! If you start small, gradually build up to fifteen minutes. Eventually, one day you'll be able to do twenty or thirty minutes a day or more and it will become a way of life.

Get started now. It's the next link to your best life!

The trick is to expect nothing.

Just do it.

Mastering silence is the first leg of a three-legged stool holding up your ability to master focus and being.

Now let's look at the second leg: mastering your intentions.

# LOOK OUT FOR YOUR UNDERLYING INTENTIONS

Your intentions are the aim that guides your actions.

When you intend to hit a target, you take the appropriate action towards it.

Therefore, becoming a master of your intentions multiplies your chances of creating what you want for yourself. We began looking at this concept with 'LYBL QUESTIONS' and limiting beliefs (see Chapters 1 and 2).

The next level covered here is to realise it is possible to want to take action on something, but having underlying intentions that can undermine the whole process or can make the action you mean to take less than effective. If you can monitor your motivation, or even your source of inspiration, and make sure it is in sync with the action you want to take, you will make the result easier to accomplish.

For this exploration, I use the words 'motivation', 'inspiration' and 'intention' interchangeably. When you have a hidden motivation or intent it can mean one of two things: either you don't even know your motivation is betraying what you are attempting to create, or a hidden motivation could be something you are aware of, but are attempting to conceal from others at all costs, at times without even knowing it.

The first kind of hidden motivation where you betray yourself could be represented as follows: let's say you want to improve your relationship with your spouse. You start taking action by being kinder and making nurturing gestures such as cooking extra-special meals or showing up with gifts. Surprisingly, you can't understand why you still want to lash out at your spouse. Soon you realise that although you think you are taking action to improve the relationship and that is what you would like, deep down you are still angry about past hurts and intend to keep punishing your partner for them. You didn't even realise there was another motivation at work.

In the second kind of hidden intention, you can have an intention or motive that you think is not obvious to anyone but you. The truth is even your hidden intentions can become obvious to others. For example, if you dislike someone, despite your best efforts to think otherwise, you may still find yourself wishing bad things for them. That is a hidden intention. Although you behave to the contrary, your underlying motivation is to not like them. You will probably still continue to behave as if this is not true, but eventually, you will do or say something that will reveal your hidden feelings.

And I have seen these at times be quite explosive by the time they occur.

The key to mastering your intentions involves facing your negative intentions. You know the ones, the ones that don't actually serve what you are trying to create. It doesn't matter how hard you work to overcome a negative intention with positive action; if the hidden negative intention is there, it will always work against you.

On the other hand, combining positive intention and positive action will achieve results. Everything must align with the positive intention in order for it to come to fruition; every thought, word and action must be congruent. Focusing your intentions so they are positive and paying attention to your subsequent actions becomes critical to unearthing your best life.

And yes! I just did a happy dance and pumped my fist in the air, because this is the type of alignment you are truly seeking!

Hidden negative intentions can be pretty tricky, so being aware of them is not that easy. They may crop up anywhere. If you become disappointed in how something is turning out, you may start unknowingly creating even more opportunities to move far away from the good thing you were trying to create. Take note of what you do, do you beat yourself up? Do you start saying that nothing ever works out for you? Do you start believing you can't or won't ever see this thing come to fruition? All of these beliefs and messages become your new intent.

In essence, this is where you start to backtrack.

And then you start to confirm and find the evidence that contributes to making it impossible for your worthy intentions to come to the forefront.

Your life will always proceed out of your intentions for it.

Similarly, if you fall back into believing negative thoughts, you plant the seeds for them to have power over you in measurable ways. You will be more likely to cling to these negative intentions than to try to turn them around in the name of something you cannot yet feel, see or touch.

# IT'S TIME TO GRAB YOUR 'LYBL' JOURNAL!

## 'LYBL' IN ACTION

### How Do Your Intentions Rate?

Here's a quick ratings overview that will assist you to decipher the quality of your intentions and have clarity around hard-to-make decisions.

Each question will uncover (or at least make you think about) whether you're harbouring any potentially damaging intentions you might not even be aware of.

1. Does this idea/action benefit me and everyone else around me?
2. Will this idea/action serve as a tool for growth instead of a weapon against me or someone else?
3. Does withholding this information or knowledge or action represent a selfless instead of a selfish act?
4. Does this idea/action grow from wisdom instead of fear or doubt?
5. Does this idea/action stem from an internal desire instead of something I feel is expected of me or put upon me by others?

Count up how many 'yes' answers you have.

The more yes's, the more pure your intention.

Pure intentions are positive and born in your wisdom.

They are more aligned with who you might ultimately want to be and also aligned with the ease with which you'll arrive where you are meant to be.

Some of the questions in this rating overview above may sound a bit out there.

I'm sure many of you can point to people who have cheated or manipulated their way to what they want, and you are pretty sure they got there without checking their true intentions.

When I think about people like that I get angry and wonder whether I should just learn to be as slippery as they are. After all, they seem to get good results right? So, I always return back to what I know - this is not who I am, therefore taking their path will only backfire.

I believe, your best bet is to keep this rating overview close at hand, because it will help you focus your intentions so you can achieve them in a way you can be proud of. Part of your accomplishments should always be a sense of pride that they are deserved and that they came to you honestly.

You can still get what you want regardless of what your intention is, but the point is to carve out wisdom so you can experience accomplishment less painfully.

Anything worth doing will challenge you and stretch you, but it doesn't need to affect your peace of mind to be worth it. By contrast, when we achieve out of negative intentions, we get what we want only at a high emotional cost.

As I watch the change that is going on with people and the choices they are making about their lives and careers, I am seeing a shift.

More and more people are judging their successes not by what they are earning or accumulating, but by what they had to give up to have it. That is what I mean by succeeding at the cost of your own peace.

So many people are no longer willing to have their success outweighed by what they sacrificed to have it. They want more time with their families, more time with themselves and time in general to enjoy their lives. That is why work/life balance is a hot topic now, as well as down sizing and people cashing in their pensions early to go and live a less stressful existence.

Of course, not all of us have the luxury, but the impetus to do so is gaining a quiet, yet forceful momentum.

I personally think it has legs and is speaking volumes to us.

Although most of my clients come to coaching for symptomatic reasons (for instance, wanting more money, to lose weight, a better career or more time with their partners or families), they almost all discover if they truly listen to their quiet voice inside, the source of their dissatisfaction is a lack of meaning, satisfaction and peace of mind.

When they find pure intention – what they truly want for themselves – their motivation is clear, so it is not difficult for them to follow through.

Finding your way to positive intentions lowers the emotional cost of succeeding.

I trust you will find the right balance here for you.

# 'LYBL' STORY: ENTER JOSH

## KNOWING YOUR POSITIVE INTENTIONS LOWERS THE EMOTIONAL COST OF SUCCESS

Josh was a family man, holding down a job, making time for his family, and doing good in his community. When he came to me for coaching, I suggested he answer the 'Intentions Rating' overview at a time when he and his family were considering moving into a bigger, more luxurious home.

When he checked his intentions against his desire for the showy home, he saw that he was being motivated by an old desire, one that had become his intention to impress his parents, colleagues and friends.

He realised he always felt he had to project the image of the perfect husband, father and provider. Suddenly, it was clear that buying the house was not an expression of himself or his family, but of a tangible reward that would then grant him the expected praise.

When Josh realised that he was being motivated by values and expectations that were actually false for him, the anxiety he had about not purchasing the house vanished. Instead, he was able to focus on making the home that his family already lived in meet all their needs in an even more satisfying way.

Taking a moment to consider his motives kept Josh from a purchase that could have been a big mistake. Buying a big house because it would make him look good, or because he felt it was expected of him, was not the foundation he wanted. He could have earned more money and afforded a big new home, but it would have been bought with false intentions. Quite possibly, if he had gone through with it he might have missed the joy this purchase was supposed to create.

# 'LYBL' STORY: MEET ANTHONY AND SOPHIE

## ARE YOU LIVING A LIFE OF ILLUSION?

Anthony and Sophie's housing challenge was the opposite of Josh's.

They had three kids, with a fourth on the way, and they were struggling to make ends meet. As we worked together on their budget, it was clear that their big, lovely home was a tremendous financial burden at the same time that it was the envy of family and friends.

It was understandable that moving to a smaller home would ease their financial pressures. Anthony and Sophie would have a substantial nest egg from the sale of the old house and a smaller mortgage, lower utility bills and so on, would create a savings of around $1,500.00 a month.

Although a move to a smaller house would create ease and financial safety in their lives, Anthony and Sophie were daunted by the prospect of having to tell the neighbours and their family and friends.

Even though they saw their intent – to create a higher quality of life – would be accomplished by this move, and one which would provide them with financial security. Staying in the big house would only be an illusion of a higher quality of life because in reality, the high expense of running the house curtailed their freedom.

With their intentions set clearly in sight, making the final decision to move was an easy choice.

I trust you are inspired to look at your intentions, for there is one more important reward you can reap by doing so. When you are a master at focusing your intentions in a positive way, they can become powerful enough to create results with less action – or sometimes even no action at all.

When you have a powerful, positive intention rooted in wisdom and not ego, you can create an even greater magnet effect than what we discussed in the last chapter.

For example, have you ever intended to get in touch with an old friend to connect and see how he or she is doing, only to bump into the friend or even a third party who could get you in touch with that friend?

Have you ever had a wish that you never really took any action towards come true?

That's the power of a big intention.

It can be something you are really attached to or may silently suffer over.

It can also be something big and perhaps improbable, and if you intend on it deeply, it can come to be.

Now, if I knew the magic formula to make this sort of thing happen over and over, I'd sell you the magic formula. All I can tell you for now is keep focused on clean, clear intentions and adjust your being to honour them.

That is how I believe great things find you.

## STAY PRESENT & FOCUSED IN YOUR OWN LIFE

Our third and last leg of mastering focus and being is in the form of focusing on your own life to find the answers to your blueprint.

So many times we stay in limbo longer than needed because we compare ourselves to others or stray from our path because of what we see someone else doing. Worry, anxiety, comparison or stress can result. Just pulling back from all the 'noise' of our daily lives can provide clarity.

By focusing on your own life, you can hear your wisdom. It may sound simple, but you can unearth the next step for you, regardless of what is going on around you.

Conventional wisdom says that when we want to accomplish something, we seek the advice of mentors or we follow the patterns of models who have achieved a similar goal already; it also suggests we become keen observers of how to accomplish what we want for ourselves.

I have noticed however, that sometimes, we can 'accidentally' overload ourselves with so much information that we have a hard time processing what is applicable and true to our own situation.

So many people are driven to distraction by looking over the fence to see what their neighbours are doing. Accepting the pace of your life and taking care of it responsibly, as we discussed in Chapter 5, will really make a difference in the long term, enabling you to get back to yourself and what you truly desire. This is what staying present and "in your own life" means.

Part of 'Your Being' and harnessing the resources of spirit includes this discipline of measuring yourself only in terms of your own life. When you spread your attention outward, gathering impressions of how life should be, you rob yourself of the wisdom your own life provides.

Learn from others, however you must keep your own centre as you layer that learning into your life.

Try not to make the mistake of abandoning your own ship.

# 'LYBL' STORY: ENTER MARIA

## STOP LOOKING OVER YOUR NEIGHBOURS FENCE

**M**aria was a very successful public relations executive. She was very unhappy but felt she was doing the right thing: in her mind, successful people worked hard and sacrificed a lot.

This was especially true for those who did not have children, like Maria herself. It was only through working with me as her coach, that she focused on her life and not on what everyone else was doing.

Once she did this, it was clear that it made sense for her to leave the big organisation she worked for and start her own business. Her new enterprise has thrived for three years without her even having to advertise or market herself.

Maria has also been under a big cloud of confusion when it came to the topics of having children. As she looked around and saw babies everywhere, she began to feel pressured and believed it was expected of her to have kids. She later admitted she stayed at her high-powered company so long in part because it was acceptable there not to have kids.

She felt she had created the image of a career woman who was riding too high on the career track to stop to have children. Once she focused on what she wanted, it was clear that kids were not actually in the picture. She no longer needed to hide behind her high-power career. She could face and accept her own truth. Maria and her husband agreed that having dogs filled their nurturing needs and that it was okay not to have kids.

# IT'S TIME TO GRAB YOUR 'LYBL' JOURNAL!

## 'LYBL' IN ACTION

### LYBL Through Questions

This is a good time to go back to your 'LYBL QUESTIONS'.

Whenever you feel pulled to compare yourself to someone else or to meet a benchmark because of what other people have accomplished, ask yourself the most powerful 'LYBL QUESTION' there is:

### "What do I want?"

Make this your mantra for several hours, or even a few days.

Don't force an answer – patiently wait for it to come to you (it will!).

The answer may not be in the form of a lightning bolt hitting you over the head; it may come as a notion or a feeling, or it could even become clear through a conversation with someone else.

It will also be particularly helpful to ask yourself what you want right before entering a period of silence.

# KEEP HOLD OF YOUR 'LYBL' JOURNAL!

## It's time to continue with your 'LYBL' Writing!

### 'LYBL' THROUGH WRITING

#### Examine Your Intentions

Take out your LYBL Journal and use this time to examine your intentions.

Look at the two or three goals or aspirations that are the most intense for you, based on all that we have covered so far.

Give yourself "The Intentions Quiz" (page 305) in writing for each one.

Write out the questions and answer them for each burning goal.

When you've uncovered your true intentions, determine whether your plans of action need to be changed.

If you discovered that the desire was not aligned with a healthy intention, change the desire to match an intention that is more positive.

Take action.

# COACHES WRAP UP

Now you've begun 'Your Being'.

This is where you begin to find the true satisfaction and peace that comes with living up to your best life. This is where we move from excavating your life blueprint to living it in harmony.

To begin, you'll need to become a master at focusing and being.

You can do this by keeping the following in mind:

- Practice silence
- Always check your true motives (your intentions)
- Change the action if you discover a negative motive
- Stay present and focused in your own life

# CHAPTER 9

# ASK FOR DIRECTIONS
# BEFORE YOU SET OUT

$\mathbf{Y}$ou're driving to a destination you haven't been to for a while, but you're sure you remember the way. After all, you have a good sense of direction and you're a great driver. You're almost there. You thought you knew your way around, but this time the roads don't seem to be in the same place they were in last time. After driving up and down the same portion of road three times, finally you decide to ask for directions.

The same thing can happen in life. You thought you knew what to do at any given time, but after driving yourself crazy trying to make something work, you gave up and started asking for help to make it work.

In either case, what if you had asked for directions or guidance before you set out the gate?

Well, for one thing, you'd probably be at your destination or somewhere even better.

Chances are that you would have saved yourself time, trouble and a great deal of energy and anxiety as well. Nobody likes being lost. By asking for guidance before you were lost, you could have spared yourself that unpleasant experience.

## YOUR INTUITION ALREADY KNOWS

$\mathbf{P}$racticing silence and mastering focus and being, opens you up to take advantage of a tremendous resource you may often overlook – your own intuition.

The messages from your intuition are the directions you may not have thought to seek out.

What is intuition anyhow? I like to think of it as knowing without knowing why you know. It goes beyond what is explainable and asks you to bring all your senses to their highest potential. After the work you did in Part Two, 'Your Actions', you are more sensitive to physical clues and more aware of your own reaction to things and the sources of those reactions.

Now you are ready to make it all come together.

Not using your intuition is a symptom of the fact that we use only a small portion of our brain. Yet, the source of intuition is not limited to your brain; it can come from other places, as you will discover.

We will also explore how to use this tremendous resource to ease your way to your life blueprint. There is always the conventional way to assess what is possible, using the five senses: sight, sound, touch, feel and smell.

And by expanding the scope of your intuition and the capacity to receive guidance in your life from a wiser, intangible part of yourself, holds the promise of saving you unnecessary steps. It can keep you on track to your best life and even be more effective than logical, linear action when it comes to achieving a goal.

Expanding your intuition will take practice.

You have to start building trust in your ability to use all the guidance available to you. It isn't easy to trust knowing without knowing why you know, but once you're successful a few times, I'm sure you won't go back to the old ways that left you lost before you asked for help.

# WHERE IS YOUR INTUITION HIDING?

There are three places your intuitive is usually hiding out: your unconscious mind, collective consciousness and the superconscious or spiritual connections.

I am going to give you good reasons to consider using these three sources of intuition as viable options for making choices in your life, if you have yet to include your intuitive side in your life. If you already do, we'll be taking your use of intuition to the next level.

What are the characteristics of each of the three sources of intuition?

**Intuition from the Unconscious**

Your unconscious mind holds all the information you've learned, acquired and experienced. When your brain is searching for an answer or guidance on something, it may look to the unconscious, the corners too obscure for your conscious self to recognise. As we focus on using our intuition, what becomes interesting is that the unconscious will take old information and form a new relationship to it. We may then use it to guide us.

Bringing up information from the unconscious is like rediscovering a forgotten possession in your garage or storage unit. It becomes new again and serves you in ways it did not before. For example, suddenly remembering a childhood story that you haven't thought of in thirty years might give you the perfect sentiment to share with a friend.

## Intuition from Collective Consciousness

Have you ever been standing in traffic, felt drawn to look at the person in the next car, and caught that person staring back at you? We are connected in our thoughts to other people, whether we choose to believe it or not. You turn your head to look into the next car because you somehow feel the other person's gaze or sense their presence.

You knew to turn *without knowing why you knew.*

When we ask for directions, sometimes we are tapping into a collective consciousness of information that comes to us in the form of an intuitive hit or understanding. Collective consciousness is the same principle that makes it possible to sometimes heal people through a prayer chain, or to think you came up with a unique, secret idea only to find your friend halfway around the world from you had the very same thought. The collective consciousness is a pool of information we can all tap into for guidance.

## Intuition from the Superconscious or the Spiritual

Whether we believe in a higher source or not, we have all admitted at one time or another that some events, coincidences and synchronicities cannot be explained by logic alone. So, if it isn't logical or rational, let's agree it came from the super conscious, the part of us in touch with what can only be reached beyond our own souls.

An intuitive notion from the superconscious, especially when you are not used to asking it for directions, will probably feel somewhat alien to you. Your intuition will probably tell you to do or say something or go somewhere that may seem out of character for you. The direction may not appear logical, but following it can have a pay-off. The prize for doing so will usually be an insight, result or idea that makes complete sense once you've heeded your intuition's direction.

I remember going on a spur of the moment getaway by myself to Fitzroy Island, situated just off the coast of Cairns. Whilst I was there, my intuition told me to abandon the planned route I had prepared for my daily hike. As uncomfortable as I was in not charting a planned course, I let my feet follow my intuition. I was not afraid, but I remember sensing a suspended reality as I let myself be guided by something intangible. As a result, I came across the most amazing beach that no one on the island had mentioned to me, and as I sat there in the silence of nature, the power of the ocean, crashing around me, I remember experiencing a beautiful yet overwhelming feeling of connection with nature and life. I was physically alone, yet felt completely at one with the universe.

Recently I have also been participating in a very simple, yet powerful form of meditation, called Kirtan. It's effortless and joyful and involves musical instruments that keep the flow of the melody and rhythm. Kirtan is an ancient Indian call and response chant practice with its roots originating from Buddhism. The ancient chants contain powerfully renewing, transformative energy that assist in a reconnection with the divinity that resides within all of us. It is a means of finding our way back to the core of our being, to our heart and to our connection with each other. After experiencing a chant session my body energetically buzzes for weeks afterwards.

It is most definitely something that I cannot explain.

It is these types of discoveries that rate as among the most magical moments in my life.

These experiences also ensure I walk away with a big lesson about the value of being flexible when it comes to any plan. I have seen and experienced how often something better than what you can plan or build can be waiting for you if you're open to it.

Intuition is as innate as the wisdom that I trust by now you believe you possess.

Some people think intuition and wisdom are virtually interchangeable.

I don't.

So let's take a minute to make the distinctions between them clear. Intuition is the data, the intuitive realisation of a possibility. Wisdom is what you do with it.

Acting on your intuition is following your own wisdom. Learning from the times your interpretation of your intuition was not quite accurate is also wisdom.

If wisdom is the memory of the soul, then intuition is the funnel of the information that empties into you for your wisdom to process. All the impressions and information comes to you through your intuition and wisdom helps you act on it.

Our journey to unearthing the blueprint to your best life has been about shedding the obstacles that keep your own wisdom at bay. One of those obstacles has been remaining unaware of your intuition. By examining how to tap into your intuition and understanding how to weave it into your life, you'll soon be able to rely on your intuition instead of ignoring it.

## BRINGING INTUITIVE GUIDANCE INTO YOUR WORLD

How do you lead a life that includes intuition and direction from less than concrete, logical sources?

Based on my own studies and experiences, I believe there are four steps that must be considered:

## Be Open to Intuition

Your work practicing silence and taking care of your life responsibly sets you up to hear what has always been lying right beneath the surface of logic and fact. When problems are at a minimum and your mind is quieter, there is room for your intuition to come through. However, you must be a believer to have it find you. Suspend judgment and trust the free fall this brings.

## Expect Intuition

Give up the notion that everything is in our control when it comes to creating your best life. Expect to co-create that life with your world by listening to its guidance. This takes the bur den off you and gives life a flow that you will begin to trust.

## Ask for Guidance from Your Intuition

Later in this chapter, I'll show you how to ask for guidance and intuitive messages in writing, but you can also do it verbally whenever you want. Ask the wiser part of you what you need to know about a specific concern or what you need to do about a specific situation. Be sensitive when waiting for an answer. It may come as something you hear, feel or see; it may even be something you interpret from a dream or that someone tells you.

I use this with something as simple as finding my keys. I ask myself, "Where are my keys?" take a deep breath and wait for what occurs to me. I usually find my keys when I follow that next thought.

And I know most of us have experienced that at some point or another!

## Act on Your Intuition

Intuitive inklings are wasted when they are not acted upon, Although they may direct you to stretch beyond your comfort zone, and even if you do not get the result you expect, acting on an inkling will help you learn about yourself. Remember, your intuition is designed for your own good. It always has your very best interests at heart.

# IT'S TIME TO GRAB YOUR 'LYBL' JOURNAL!

## 'LYBL' IN ACTION

### Raise Your Awareness

The best way to start you off using your intuition or to take it to the next level is to raise your awareness to the point where you start noticing every thought that occurs to you.

You can begin by taking a day or you can work on this for a week or even longer, whatever takes your fancy!

Every time you have a thought or an inclination to call someone, do something, wear something or try something, I want you to do it.

It is paramount to remember these inklings of intuition will seem free of emotion and will feel very neutral.

If what occurs to you is destructive in any way – eating that extra dessert, telling someone what you really think of them, cheating your way around a problem – then it is not your intuition trying to speak to you. Those are negative thoughts that don't count for this activity.

To come to trust your intuition, track what occurs to you, act on the positive inklings, (even if they don't make sense), and watch which ones result in helpful guidance. Even an inkling to wear a favourite piece of jewellery might become significant when it becomes a great conversation-starter with someone you've been eager to meet and you finally get the chance on this particular day.

The difference between this process and the 'Blank Day' exercise in Chapter 4 is that this one goes further.

Now you are going beyond what you want, to a point where you are allowing intuitive guidance to lead you to something out of your conscious awareness that might be best for you.

# IS FEAR GETTING IN THE WAY OF YOUR INTUITION?

We established earlier that fear is the greatest obstacle to any wisdom trying to reach us. The same holds true with intuition. In order to act on intuition, you'll need to distinguish between the intuition itself and when fear is getting in the way.

Fear can often talk to you in harsh ways. Intuition would never do that. Even if you don't listen to intuition first, it will always linger in the gentlest of ways. Maybe a nagging feeling would be intuitive guidance at its worst, but it would not get worse than that. Intuition will always be gentle, fear will not.

For example, being afraid to fly in an airplane might give you the jitters, make you anxious and upset for days before a trip, or even evolve dreams of nightmarish terror with associated planes and flying. But if your intuition were trying to send you a warning and directing you to not go on a plane, it would nudge you to change the reservation or you'd get the feeling that you'd better go on this trip another time. Intuition, will not terrorise you, it will direct you.

# 'LYBL' STORY: ENTER SALLY

## WHEN INTUITION COMES KNOCKING – BE READY!

Sally had done everything "right" – attended a good university, found a good job as a scientist, been singled out for praise at the corporation where she worked – and yet harboured a secret dissatisfaction with her life. She longed for a more extroverted career, specifically as a trainer, teaching adults in corporations.

However, Sally's scientifically trained mind, used to needing proof and concrete evidence, would not allow her to make the leap to follow her desire.

When she was about to be promoted again, Sally hired me as a coach under the pretence of wanting to start her new job off on the right foot.

It didn't take long to uncover her dream of changing careers, but it took a lot of prodding before she would take action. It wasn't until an 'inexplicable' depression started to set in that Sally was willing to explore the possibility of moving on to what was calling her.

Sally finally accepted my suggestion that she enquire about the requirements to be come an in-house trainer. The training director echoed all her rational doubts: "You have no background in training. You have to at least take some courses. You need experience." Sally retreated, feeling a strange mix of rejection and satisfaction, the latter from knowing she had been justified in suppressing this desire.

The very same week, Sally, 'coincidentally' met a man at her gym, named Peter. A trainer for a large consulting firm, he also volunteered at a program that taught life skills to inner-city kids.

Intrigued, she expressed interest in helping with the program, but when Peter called to follow up, she backed away from making a commitment.

Within two weeks of this happening Sally found herself lost in an unfamiliar part of the city and pulled into a crowded school parking lot to find someone to ask directions. And of course, lo and behold, who did she see but Peter. On his way to lead one of his classes for the kids, he invited her to take a peek.

Intrigued by seeing the program in action, this time Sally actually volunteered to help with administration. As a result, she got a chance to observe the course several times. One Saturday, Peter called Sally from this car; he was stuck in a huge traffic jam, and he was not going to make it to the kids' course on time, if at all. He begged Sally to take his place. Despite her initial resistance, Sally felt she had no choice but to lead the class.

As it turned out, Sally was a hit – the kids loved her. Peter invited Sally to lead the class as often as she wanted to. He was very impressed with her warmth and her natural teaching abilities. Buoyed by his praise and inspired by watching how well Peter could work with adults and kids, Sally once more felt encouraged to pursue her dreams of becoming a trainer.

About six months later, Peter recommended Sally to his boss. She interviewed for a position at Peter's company, and he promised to be available to mentor her. Sally was offered the trainer's job, and quickly accepted. She was on her way.

Sally's intuition about changing careers was more stubborn than she was.

Once she admitted the truth about what she wanted, she was unleashing wisdom.

Despite the fact that she was resistant to taking action, the path to her fulfilment found her. The coincidences involved – meeting Peter at the gym, running into him in the inner city – were life's way of guiding her until she could no longer deny her life blueprint.

And I know as you reflect on Sally's story that you are already thinking of a number of your own situations or stories that you are aware of that are very similar, be it with yourself or involving friends and family members.

# NOT ALL GUIDANCE WILL BE LITERAL

Learning to distinguish intuition from fear will increase your intuitive hits.

You'll also become better and better at interpreting some of the less literal messages your intuitive guidance is trying to deliver. Very few people will receive the kind of guidance that involves hearing very real, distinct voices or seeing images in their mind telling them what to do.

People with that level of sensitivity move into psychic spheres of clairvoyance.

For most of us, it will usually come in the form of a thought, a feeling or a dream.

It may even be something more obviously attention-grabbing, such as five people telling you to read the same book, until you finally get the message and succumb to the purchase.

Not all guidance will be literal.

Some you may have to interpret. This will mean recognising some of the less obvious signs that your intuition is trying to reach you. These signs will often be symbolic.

For example, a friend of mine, Julie, has a strong symbolic attachment to butterflies. They remind her of her father who has passed away, because her father had such a huge love for them.

Not only is she reminded of him, but also depending on what is going on in her life at the time, a butterfly can represent that her father is sending guidance.

It seems a strong coincidence that whenever she's confused about something, she may notice a butterfly in a garden, or a picture of one in a magazine or hanging somewhere in a café. It doesn't matter what form it comes in, but when she sees a butterfly of any kind, it symbolically reminds her of her dad. It also makes her consider what he would say about the dilemma. This is usually enough to jog her out of the confusion and into clarity. The symbol reminds her to run in to herself and the answer.

Similarly, for me, the simple raising of hairs on my arm and an energetic vibration I have external to me tells me symbolically that I have heard or spoken the truth.

When that happens, I know not to ignore what was just said, but to pay special attention to it, and to proceed from that realisation to the course of action it is directing me to take.

# IT'S TIME TO GRAB YOUR 'LYBL' JOURNAL!

## 'LYBL' IN ACTION

### Symbolic Benchmarks

Take notice of any symbols you have come to recognise in your life as meaningful. If you do not have any, keep this in the forefront of your attention for a couple of days trying to notice things that seem significant to you in terms of guidance.

They will usually represent positive impressions instead of negative ones.

I trust you realise I am not talking about superstition. No black cats or rabbits feet.

I want to guide you to find symbolic benchmarks that will assist to heighten your own trust in your intuition.

The symbols are highly personal and only you can recognise them.

They are like pats on the back from your intuition, which say, "Yep, you're on the right track."

Look for them and start using them whatever they may be, whatever area of your life they may come from.

# DON'T BECOME A SLAVE TO INTUITION

There is such a thing as going too far with interpreting your intuition and the meaning of everything that happens to you.

Don't become a slave to intuition.

That's the same as believing your doctor, your tarot card reader or your child's teacher is always right.

Intuition is not exact science, and your intuitive inklings are open to interpretation.

Your interpretation won't always be right (although you'll get better at hearing it and receiving it over time) and not everything has to have huge significance.

Sometimes things just are the way they are because they are.

If trying to come up with an interpretation of an event or inkling or dream causes you to suffer or get down on yourself, stop! Don't force it. Guidance is supposed to be gentle (if you need that lesson reinforced, go back to our discussion of entering 'the zone' on page 169).

If an answer or an interpretation is not forthcoming, give it time – it might turn up later, when you least expect it, or not at all.

Use what you have learned in this chapter to enhance your life, not to make it more complicated.

# IT'S TIME TO GRAB YOUR 'LYBL' JOURNAL!

## 'LYBL' THROUGH WRITING

### Ask Your Wiser Mind

This writing connection will be different from anything we've done so far, but that is because it comes in the advanced part of the journey toward your best life.

Until now you've explored things in writing, maybe even written a letter to yourself. Now we are going to raise the bar on heightening your intuitive sense by writing to a wiser part of you. You can call it higher self, your wise mind, or whatever resonates with you.

Using 'LYBL QUESTIONS' again, address a challenge you would like guidance on by asking your wiser mind questions. Do this exercise with only one challenge at a time. It can be about anything that is frustrating you or about the specific meaning of an event in your life. If you need assistance, consult the list of 'LYBL QUESTIONS' in Chapter 1, or even flick back through your LYBL Journal to rediscover them.

Write to your wise mind until you have asked all your questions and expressed all your frustrations about the challenge.

"What do I need to know about dealing with X?" you may ask. Or, "What am I overlooking to make this happen? Or, "What good is supposed to come out of the anger I feel about X?"

Continue asking until you feel ready to hear an answer. Then take a moment to breathe deeply and clear those questions of any emotions with another deep breath. When you feel you are in a neutral place emotionally, pick up your pen again.

Now let your wise mind write back. You may think that you are making up the answers you want to hear, however keep writing.

Simply write what occurs to you.

Write until you feel you have nothing else to say.

When you read what you've written, there should be nuggets of wisdom for you to act on or contemplate.

If not, do not throw them away. Often time will be your greatest measure as to the accuracy of your wise mind's predictions and answers.

I am constantly amazed that when I do this style of writing, that what I have written months later always resonates with the guidance I received from my very own self was true, productive and sometimes even tends to appear as a miracle.

Notice the voice that speaks back to you in the writing.

You will notice it to be more kind and caring than the inner critic you may have.

Many of my retreat program participants have talked about the lack of punishing, negative voice and how they feel they've found a friend in themselves through this writing.

Use this activity as often as you like to tap into the wiser part of you, you know, the one that already knows.

For many, it becomes a daily ritual, and one that I most certainly highly recommend.

# COACHES WRAP UP

**B**y using intuition to ask for directions and guidance before you set out or need help, you can tap into all the resources available to you as you become more attuned to your blueprint and its payoff of a happy, fulfilled life.

- Raise your awareness and notice what occurs to you
- Be open to intuition
- Ask for guidance from it
- Act on your intuition
- Recognise symbols that intuitive clues are trying to reach you
- Write to your wise mind regularly

# CHAPTER 10

# EMBRACE YOUR
# UNCERTAINTY

$W$hat do you need to know to have the life that you want?

Do you need to know how to make a living?

Do you need to know how to be a loving parent?

Do you need to know how to make a million dollars?

What is it that you feel you must know in order to get what you want?

Let me answer for you.

You do not need to know anything specifically. You just need to know that you have the inner authority to not let yourself down.

So many people feel they cannot have what they want until they get another degree, become fully accomplished in something, or are absolutely certain of what they want out of their life.

These however, are not prerequisites for success, satisfaction or happiness. In fact, knowledge can be limited – it can hinder possibility.

If you know women only make 0.75 cents to the dollar that men earn on average, then you may find yourself defined and limited by that fact. You may not ask for more, even though you feel you deserve it, or may limit yourself in some other way.

Yes, sometimes ignorance can be bliss.

If I had known that my first book, 'Bringing Life To Leadership' was in a book genre that normally is not expected to exceed sales of twenty-five thousand copies, I would never have dreamed of selling a million copies.

Not, that I have reached that number – yet – but book sales went way above what was expected, because of my dedication to making the book sell, my social media presence, my heart and soul efforts, and because I did not know any better. Because I didn't know any better, I did everything I could to make that book sell, and it did.

We grasp our knowledge because we have been trained to believe that knowledge is power and with that power we hope to find security.

This is another major stumbling block to wisdom that wants to come through to guide your life. The greatest security comes in trusting yourself enough to not be phased by the unknown. We will look at that true security in this final section of our work on 'Your Being'.

Creativity can be described as letting go of certainty.

Not knowing gives us the freedom to create.

If I were to guess at the thing that keeps people the most dissatisfied with their lives it would be the loss of their creativity or the feeling they are not making any progress.

Whether it's their marriage, their relationship, their job, their health or life in general, when things become mundane – when we have fallen into a routine and are merely doing what we know – we lose that spark that gives our lives wings.

My very first coach said to me, "'I don't know, is a great opportunity for creativity."

One of my mentors, Sharon Pearson has always told me that the person with the most behavioural flexibility will always win; I have always related this to embracing moments of uncertainty.

So finding the wisdom in uncertainty gives us the experience of ourselves that we long for. We are creative beings. When we experience the power of creating something where there was nothing before, we feel a tremendous sense of power.

That power – not the power of the knowledge, but the power of creating our own lives from the fibre of our own being – is our creative life force.

When we cling to the notion that knowledge is the only way we can have that power, we lessen what we are capable of. Knowing or knowledge can also lead to prejudice and snobbery, both of which paralyse parts of us. You may miss out on a fulfilling friendship or experience because you have prejudged the outcome by thinking you know the reputation of the person you're about to meet or the reputation of the company you might have been thinking of joining.

Thinking you know can make you jaded.

Think of going to see a revival of a famous Broadway play. If it's a classic you've read or seen before, why go? Perhaps you would go to discover nuances you might have missed, to pick up something unexpected, or to be open to a new interpretation by the director or the actors. Not knowing and just going for the ride is a huge part of reaching the satisfaction and fulfilment of your life blueprint.

I'm not advocating that you forget everything you've ever learned and become a blank slate. Without my recent years of knowledge, I most probably might not be where I am now.

The knowledge that you've gained is an integral part of you and the certain skills you've been taught, such as how to cook, are highly desirable things to hold onto.

For the exploration of this chapter, the blueprint you need to excavate isn't always rooted in what you know, and a lack of knowledge shouldn't be used as an excuse for not taking action on what you desire.

As you explore the concept of not needing to know, you will realise how much you rely on what you know instead of using who you are to make a difference.

The payoff to relying more on who you are than on what you know includes deeper relationships, more innovative solutions to everyday problems and an increased sense of self.

# IT'S TIME TO GRAB YOUR 'LYBL' JOURNAL!

## 'LYBL' IN ACTION

### Be Comfortable with Not Knowing

To start you on the way to being comfortable with not knowing, spend the next twenty-four hours free of having answers.

In other words, refuse to be the expert on anything for a day.

Refrain from answering any query you're asked, be it by your kids, work colleagues, spouse, or even your own self.

When appropriate, respond with: "I'll have to get back to you on that."

Or ask the person a question that will help them to come up with the answer themselves (refer back to your 'LYBL QUESTIONS').

Or, instead of jumping in with an answer, ask them what they think the answer is. You will be amazed at how many times the other person can answer their own question if given the chance.

Regardless of how you deflect the question, the point is for you to experience the enquiry that ensues when you allow yourself to 'not know'.

Notice how you behave differently.

Notice how you feel.

Notice how your creativity and conversation with others change.

Does it make you feel more secure or insecure to now know?

Record your impressions in your LYBL Journal.

# 'LYBL' STORY: ENTER TROY

## THRIVE IN UNCERTAIN TIMES

Troy had a very nice position at a large well-known organisation in Australia and loved the people he worked with.

He had a good salary, he was well liked, and he had been promoted a number of times, but he felt something was missing and that his creativity had been shut down by the routine and lack of challenge.

When we started working together, Troy found that helping others and contributing to the development of people was the part of his work he enjoyed the most. However, he did this for only part of his day, and that wasn't enough for him to feel fully alive at his job.

I introduced Troy to one of my favourite organisations, a for purpose not for profit group that assists young people between the ages of ten to eighteen to have a better future, so that he might fulfil his need to help others.

Troy did not know how to coach or how to deal with youth, but it appealed to him so he trained to be a volunteer coach.

During his training, as he observed how everyone in the group was respectful and really believed in its mission, he felt compelled to get more involved.

Before he even knew what had come his way, Troy had taken a sabbatical from his full-time job, on half pay.

He wasn't sure how he would make ends meet, but he felt he could afford the risk. By the time six months were even up, he found himself in a conversation with the Executive Director at the youth organisation about becoming its next leader, he had heard that she was preparing to change her role.

The position was unlike anything he had done before, nor did he know much about non-profits, but Troy decided to leave his job to assume the Executive Director position.

He now tells me he feels energised and has a sense of purpose in all he does each day at work.

Troy is not sure what the future holds, but he is on the board of several start-up businesses, is training to improve his coaching skills, and has a plan he thinks will work for him.

The people around him have told him he seems happier, he and his girlfriend have got engaged, and his family and friends are supporting him like they never have before.

Not knowing what was coming was the perfect way for Troy to begin to discover how to live his best life.

## LEAP AND THE NET WILL APPEAR

Some say that the leap of faith is necessary to believe, to do, or to be, but you don't need to become a great thinker to realise anything worth having, doing, or even being takes a leap of faith to get to.

Giving up the need to know also includes taking leaps of faith.

You may not be sure of an outcome, but you can trust the decision to move forward if you know you'll somehow land on your feet.

Having a difficult conversation with someone, starting a business from scratch or changing careers in midlife are all courageous moves that require leaps of faith.

What is keeping you from taking a leap of faith? For most of us, it is that common enemy, fear.

Let's take a moment to put some structure around deciding whether to take a leap of faith or not.

How do you know when it's okay to not know what the outcome will be, and still take a leap of faith?

## WISDOM WILL ALWAYS PULL YOU; IT WILL NEVER PUSH YOU

When it comes to leaps of faith, things that call to you, that propel you, or that somehow pull you towards them seem to work out better than things you are pushing to make happen.

Wisdom will always pull you; it will never push you.

You need to let yourself feel the subtle difference between pushing for a result and being pulled to accomplish one.

Many of my clients have questions about this concept.

How do you want something and yet not push for it?

Does that mean you don't go after it?

Does that mean you pretend you don't want it?

Does that mean let the other person or parties make the first move?

The answer to these last three questions is a resounding "no", and it doesn't mean you should settle or sit in your room and visualise it into existence, either.

The way to get something without pushing for it is to take appropriate action, and at the same time, watch yourself to make sure you're not trying too hard.

If you find yourself scheming, plotting or second-guessing yourself and everyone else, as well as attempting to manipulate a situation in your favour, you are pushing.

The energy it takes to push for a result chokes the faith out of any leap, and makes it hard, although not impossible, to get results.

It simply takes great effort and often there's no sense of enjoyment in the doing.

It becomes difficult because of fear. You are afraid that you won't ultimately lead your best life without this thing, so you try to manipulate your world to make it happen.

On the other hand, if you feel pulled by something or moved to passionately pursue something even against great odds and obstacles, keep going.

As long as you are not hurting yourself or anyone else in the process, it is wisdom prodding you, when you are pulled by something, it will usually be something that has a greater purpose than your own material satisfaction.

Even if it is not, it most likely allows for the kind of personal fulfilment that is in itself a great contribution to your world. Often, taking a stand for the better part of yourself – or for something that serves more than your purposes – allows for the magical results that defy explanation.

The leap of faith is rewarded.

A leap of faith requires not knowing what the result will be.

It is a dance.

The perfect dance partner doesn't step on their partner's toes. If your partner is attempting to control you instead of lead you, they will definitely make it an erratic dance. The perfect dance partner stands awaiting the cue and responding in an imperceptible second. That is the dance of pull. You need to be the ideal partner.

# EVEN WHEN YOU ARE <u>NOT</u> DOING YOUR BEST, YOU <u>ARE</u> DOING YOUR BEST

Am I being lazy, or is it really not the right time?

That is what I hear when things aren't going exactly as someone planned. There is really only so much we can control and when we know we have done our best to make something happen, then all we can do is wait.

That is the hardest part.

Coming to know the difference between waiting patiently for something to happen and being lazy is a big part of being comfortable with not knowing and developing a trust in yourself.

My first coach told me, "Even when you are not doing your best, you are doing your best." I interpreted this to mean that although I know I have done better, if this is all I can do now, it is the best I can do for now.

That may sound like a nice positive spin to get yourself off the hook, but there is no question that forgiving yourself for your momentary lapse in excellence is much more productive than constantly hanging shit on yourself.

The standard I recommend is taking an honest look at the effort you've made.

If you have done everything you can think of (including getting outside, additional support) to approach a project or a desired outcome, then it is time to let it rest.

Let the power of that effort have some time to mature.

Maybe you'll find a better way later, or maybe it was meant to show you something else about yourself but never came to fruition.

If you are not in action, and if you are hiding from what you say you want, then you are sabotaging your efforts.

You know deep down when fear is getting the best of you. Break the goal down to a bite-size piece that you can chew off now.

The other possible approach would be to re-evaluate your goal to ensure it is really something you truly want. If it doesn't feel that way, the desired outcome may very well be something you felt you should do.

And I can tell you now, leaps of faith cannot come from 'should'.

# 'LYBL' STORY: ENTER ANNA

### BEING PULLED? THEN, START NOW

When Anna attended one of my retreat programs, she was between jobs and thinking and feeling like she needed to get a temp job. Anna had a great sense of design and a dream to produce unusual greeting cards from photographs she had collected. She had neither business experience nor a lot of money, but she felt pulled to her idea and she felt the time to start was now.

Many of Anna's friends and family thought she was crazy for taking such a big chance, she was determined however to not let the naysayers stop her. She was scared and she was flirting with financial disaster, yet, she still chose to go full steam ahead.

In a few months, she had designed her entire line of cards, had them placed in shops and was selling them online through her website.

Today, her business is still in the start-up stage, and is growing steadily.

Although logic would dictate that Anna could have reduced the risk by taking a temp job, and she herself will admit she had no guarantee of a positive outcome, she trusted herself and knew that even if she failed, she'd find a way through it.

That attitude and confidence is the way of wisdom and the fuel that accelerates the blueprint to your best life.

# IT'S TIME TO GRAB YOUR 'LYBL' JOURNAL!

## 'LYBL' IN ACTION

### There is No Time Like the Present

Here is a cliché you can really use: there is no time like the present.

Put down this book and take one action towards something you've always wanted to do.

It doesn't have to be a major life-changing leap of faith; it can be something as simple as a new hairstyle, learning a new sport, hobby or skill, or anything that you have had stuck on the back burner or glaring at you from your vision board.

Whatever it is, trust that there is some reason you are drawn to it and do it now; make a move towards doing it.

Once you do, take a moment to observe what you learned from what you did or attempted to do.

You wouldn't think that finally trying golf would radically alter your life, but there could be more to learn from it than the mechanics of the game. You may find that you can push yourself physically further than you thought, or that you are better at strategy than you believed.

These insights are the wisdom gained from taking that particular leap.

Trust that there is a reason you were drawn to it, regardless of how practical it may be.

For instance, I once participated in a ceremonial firewalk. On my first attempt walking the coals barefoot, I got burnt. I was determined to do it again because I didn't intend to do another ceremony like this again. The leader asked me to walk this time for "something bigger than yourself". I silently decided to walk for the generations who would benefit because of my legacy and message being passed on over and over again in this lifetime. I sailed across the coals as if I were elevated a metre above them.

This was not something I need to do again, but as a leap of faith, it made me understand the power of using your life for something bigger than your goals.

In that way, the one-time experience of fire-walking has shaped my life since.

> Regardless of what you reach to do, record your impressions of your experience in your LYBL Journal so you can reflect on it as you journey closer and closer towards your best life.

# LET GO OF CONTROL

At some point during this work we are doing together, I trust you started to feel a bit lost. As you evolve toward the life you are meant to live, you may start feeling a bit disoriented because you've begun to let go of controlling every aspect of what happens to you.

That is how you know you are living in your human "beingness" versus your human "doingness".

The purpose of this book is to assist you to grow beyond the life you think you want in order to live your best life.

The wisdom that comes from giving up the need to know allows you to move more freely toward that best life. Not knowing speeds up the evolution of your life and yourself because there is no preconceived notion to struggle with.

You look at responsibility differently.

You build a strong foundation by getting your life to work, as you've done throughout the course of this book, so you are then able to let go, expecting the best and yet well prepared to endure the worst.

Preparing your life for success this way reminds me of how actors prepare for a play. For the intense period of rehearsals, they learn their lines, work out their movements on the stage with their fellow actors, live and breathe the text.

On opening night, however, they let go.

Confident that they've done their homework, they forget all the details of the weeks of rehearsal. Now the performance belongs to the synchronicity of the moment. The actors have their technique and the experience of rehearsals as their foundation, but the best performance happens in the moment.

And so does your best life.

After doing the work in these three stages of unearthing your life blueprint, you are poised for your best life.

You've done the work, you've set the stage and now you let 'Your Being' part of you take over.

You've now stepped into the power you have to create your own life.

# IT'S TIME TO GRAB YOUR
# 'LYBL' JOURNAL!

## 'LYBL' THROUGH WRITING

### Who Are You Now?

This is the last writing activity of our present journey together.

Simply write about your impressions of who you are now compared to who you were when you began this book.

Also, take a moment to look at your first writing entry, about where you were in your life and what you were hoping to accomplish.

Have your arrived?
Is the aim completely different?
What have you learned?
How did you grow?

Chances are your goals have also changed by now, or at least they've changed their meaning and significance?

# COACHES WRAP UP

**W**hen you give up needing to know and are able to embrace moments of uncertainty, you have reached the ultimate level of trust in yourself.

Here are some tips to keep in mind as you integrate this strategy into your life.

- Value creativity and possibility over knowledge
- Practice not knowing by asking more questions
- Measure the pull against the push and take a leap of faith
- When being pulled or called, get started
- Measure laziness against patience and trust in perfect timing
- Do what you want to do and watch what you learn

*"Knowledge is proud that it has learned so much.*
*Wisdom is humble that it knows no more."*

# IN REFLECTION

# YOUR AWAKENING, YOUR ACTIONS, YOUR BEING: LIVE YOUR BEST LIFE

How will you know if you are living your life blueprint?

The simple answer is that you'll be happy and feel tremendous gratitude for your life, even if you are still working towards your dreams.

If that doesn't give you enough information there are other ways to assist you to determine whether you have reached the point of living your best life.

Ask yourself these questions:

- Am I future and solution oriented, instead of past and problem focused?

- Do I catch myself falling into negative beliefs and know how to reverse them?
- Do I have more satisfying relationships because I keep conflict in perspective?
- Do I recognise the unacceptable and take immediate action to change it?
- Am I aware of how I make a difference in the world, regardless of my life's status or job description?
- Do I have more than enough time for things that really matter to me?
- Am I attracting opportunities, seemingly without effort?
- Can I move through challenges and problems with more ease?
- Am I taking chances? Ones that move my life forward in a positive way?
- Do I have deep respect for who I am and design my life to suit myself?

If the majority of your answers are yes, good on you, you are well on the way to living your life blueprint.

You've now entered a whole dimension in living – living your best life.

You've progressed through 'Your Awakening', 'Your Actions', and 'Your Being', and if you've read this book in the manner in which I intended you have, it should deliver you to where you are meant to be.

Only you can know if you've arrived there, although, if you set a preconceived notion of what this should be, you probably found you were wrong.

Sometimes, you have to give up the dream of your life to have the life of your dreams.

Which means we often don't know where we are meant to be until we arrive there.

Your best life (where you are meant to be) is a life where you can take the good with the bad, experience a lot of love and feel that you are fully expressed in the world without being anyone or anything other than your truest self.

As you commit to following the strategies in this book, you will arrive at your best life by creating the circumstances by which great things can find you.

Letting these things in requires being specific about what you want, what is ideal for you, and what must be let go from your present life to have those things.

Being open to these things also requires detachment of being open to something greater and possibly even more than what you can imagine.

The process that we have undergone together takes work and is an ongoing evolution. I recommend you come back to this book for a reference course in your wisdom whenever you may feel tested and challenged.

It will be particularly powerful if you feel you've lost your centre – as we often can when life throws at us a completely new set of circumstances. These obstacles are also part of the blueprint, and the more you practice this work, the easier and faster you will get back on track to your best life.

To maintain what you've accomplished here on our journey together, keep these things in mind.

- We were all born whole, complete and perfectly how we need to be
- Be responsible for your thoughts, words and actions
- Decide who you want to be before deciding what you'll do
- Co-operate with your world by taking action
- Be grateful for what is (even if you don't like it)
- Behave as if the results have already arrived

Act for yourself.

Think for yourself.

Implement your innate creativity.

Allow your wisdom to drive you.

And always remember, we are all born with all we need inside us in order to go about living our very best life.

After doing the work in this book, this will not be an issue for you. You are now aware that being wired for wisdom makes you able to find the answers to your life's queries. You are more able to adjust to the rapid change that surrounds you in today's world.

By now, I trust you have stopped asking yourself, "How can I have it all?" and have started to ask "What do I really want?" and my desire is that you are taking action accordingly. When you know what you want, you narrow the focus of your life to a portion that is manageable and where your success can breed more of itself.

You've probably already noticed that I haven't delivered you to some magical nirvana, as if this book was to be your magic pill.

What I do know, is that you've started to experience the magic of doing what feels right and of having your world respond positively.

Satisfaction, happiness, fulfilment and a meaningful life need not be difficult to find. They are inherent to the wisdom you already possess; you need only decide to have them and to make the wisest choices to activate and protect them. You now have the tools to access your wisdom and therefore the fulfilment, meaning, satisfaction and happiness you desire.

It is up to you to decide how hard you will make it for yourself.

I used to believe that only by doing three hours a day of aerobic exercise would I achieve the perfect body. Because I believed that, that is what it took. Now I believe that yoga, stretching and meditation keep my body in ideal condition, and they do. I redirected the level of intensity of my exercise regime from high impact to low impact, without giving up on wonderful results.

Similarly, you need to make a choice whether you will stay in the craziness or find your satisfaction another way. I am not by any means suggesting you drop out or give up. Committing to your best life means finding the speed and activity level that suits you, and then making the rest of the world cooperate around it.

We truly live in an amazing time.

A time where I believe we are better off breaking the rules than keeping them. A time where we are free to design our own lives based on our own wisdom without great fear of retribution. We are not called witches or radicals or hippies these days, so play that to your advantage.

So many rules you live by are perceived expectations you have placed on yourself. Get out and be free. You hold the key to your own best life, and you always have.

You've begun to think differently now. Give yourself permission to follow your own wisdom to your happiness.

As your coach, I insist on it and will stand for nothing less.

Be your own coach now, and accept nothing but the very best for yourself.

It will change your life.

Go on, I dare you.

I dare you to 'Live Your Best Life™'.

# GRATITUDE FOR YOU, THE READER

It is simple, I write FOR YOU.

I serve, FOR YOU.

I coach, FOR YOU.

You are ALL the inspiration behind my company name, the meaning behind it and the love I have for it.

And everyday I know you are there, I feel you.

Every day I think of you.

I feel you taking action everyday and I honour who you are.

So, before our current journey together closes as you near the end of this book, I wanted to personally thank you for trusting me to be your guide on your journey to live your best life.

Thank you also for being a part of my journey as an author, speaker and coach and for bringing to life all that I do.

Everything you need to live your best life is already inside you, so listen and keep connected to your wisdom so that you always continue to do just that.

Go on! You know you deserve it!

Live Your Best Life……always.

More than much love to you.

Michele

☺

P.S. I love Facebook messages or e-mails from fellow 'Live Your Best Lifer's' out there living their best lives, so if you feel the desire to send me a note to let me know how you are living your best life, please do so, I'd love to hear from you.

michele@foryoucorporation.com

# BE A PART OF THE 'LYBL' COMMUNITY

Now that you are well on your way and feeling inspired to live your best life, check out our range of
'Live Your Best Life™' products and merchandise to uplift you on your journey.

**www.lybl-liveyourbestlife.com**

We would love to hear how you are living your best life, so keep us posted as to how LYBL brings sunshine to your world.

Join our LYBL Community on Facebook:
**LYBL – Live Your Best Life**
&
Follow us on Instagram
**lybl_liveyourbestlife**

**#liveyourbestlife**
Share your stories and photos with the LYBL community to keep us all focused on the greater good.

Be a part of the global
**"Live Your Best Life™"** movement today ☺

# CONNECT WITH ME ONLINE

**Personal website:**

http://michelejones.com/

**Corporate website:**

http://foryoucorporation.com/

**Facebook – Public Figure:**

https://www.facebook.com/michelejones4U

**Facebook – Personal:**

https://www.facebook.com/michele.jones.7967

**You Tube:**

https://www.youtube.com/user/MicheleJones4U

**LinkedIn:**

https://www.linkedin.com/in/michelejones4u

**Instagram:**

https://instagram.com/lybl_liveyourbestlife

# ACKNOWLEDGEMENTS

# THANKS FOR SHARING IN THE JOURNEY

This book would not be possible without my clients, retreat participants, workshop, seminar, keynote audiences and blog readers who allow me the privilege of working with them on their lives.

Thank you for your trust and for being willing to share your experiences with me. It is such an honour to journey together, to learn together and to grow together.

To all the "Live Your Best Life™" Graduates and all who have been a part of the retreat program's success to date, you are the life force for the mission and everyday I am grateful that you are a part of the 'Live Your Best Life™' revolution and movement. Together we are pioneering this belief and philosophy all around the world. Thank you for paying it forward and for loving the vision as much as me.

Especially a huge hug of love and thanks to the "Live Your Best Life™" Crew Members and Ambassadors who everyday are beside me and within me creating the magic we get to, and together we get to shine our lights for others and that is pretty special. Thank you for believing in me and for not only sharing the vision and being on the mission with me, but also for creating it and evolving it together because of all you bring and offer to this world, you are all wonderful, unique and hold a very dear and special place in my heart – from my heart to your heart as awesome Coaches I honour you, Sheree Burman, Tara Davidson and Dave Thompson and all my support team and crew, Dave Wilkinson, Cathy Jones, Chris Davidson, Paul Morgan, Vernon Savage, Clint Kopittke and Nathan Evans.

Thank you for all that you bring to the program and also for our strong bond and connections as friends. Individually we are one drop, together we are an ocean. I look forward to all that lies ahead together and all that we will continue to create.

A special mention most certainly must go to my 'Big Business Club' members – be it the 'Big Business Best Life Club', 'Big Business Breakfast Club', 'Big Business Leadership Club' or the 'Big Business Mastermind Club', you are all amazing and provide me with the driving force to continually deliver for you. Thanks for your belief in me so that together we can achieve great things. There are no words to describe how I feel when I play witness to your personal development and growth, and the results you achieve.

To the main 'Dude' and creator of the SpiritCast Network and the Inspirational Book writer's Retreat, Mr., 'Living Outrageously' Dave Thompson, you are right up there with coconuts my friend! Thank you for saying 'yes', believing it could be done and for creating the space and environment, which not only allows people to deliver their messages to the world, but provides them with all they need to connect to their spirit, so that they come in spirit. I love creating with you, I am extremely grateful for our friendship and the honour it is to serve the world with you. I look forward to many things to come and know that there will be big things ahead.

And to all the Inspirational Book writer's Retreat Authors and Crew Members, how awesome that we get to share in this together. Thank you for all your support and for all that we represent as a group. I love that we champion one another and pave the way for others to follow.

Benjamin Reeves…you continue to be a beacon of light on this planet, goose bumps to know that your heart has been set free and now has permission to soar. Keeping moving forward my friend.

To my Editor, Maria Martello ☺ Thank you for everything you bring to the table, ensuring that this book made it from manuscript and into printed pages. And my apologies that somehow along the line, I managed to triple my word count from book # 1! I trust you enjoyed the read and could feel me speaking directly to you.

To my many mentors, guides and healers throughout my lifetime – Shane Ward, Sharon Pearson, Chris Niarchos, Paul Burkett, Alice Haemmerle, Joe Pane, Rachel Anastasi, Dave Thompson, Tony Robbins, Oprah Winfrey, Simon Sinek, Seth Godin, Ginny Clarke, Dorothy (Dot) James, Lyne McDonald,

Deb Wallace, Brian Bloomer, Judy McWilliams – thank you for leading the way by sharing your own insights and passion with the world, whilst providing a great modelling platform for my own evolution to take flight; allowing the ripple effect of your message to continue as a lot of all you have provided now lives within me.

And of course my inner circle of friends and family, you challenge me, encourage me; support me in so many ways, speaking always directly to my heart. I thank you especially in the time when you think I may have completely lost the plot with another crazy, whacky idea! Thank you for being on my team and for making my world a better place. It is your gentle resolute encouragement to persist that at times keeps me going.

To my mother, Lois Flanagan, for so many things I thank you, for all the sacrifices you have ever made for me as child, to ensure a roof over our heads, food on the table, braces on my teeth, my black pants for drama that I simply had to have for Mr. Carroll's drama class, a life of adventure, and all the wonderful times we have spent together connecting as mother and daughter. I know at times, you wish I would slow down and not be so 'busy', yet I believe my get up and go for life was genetically passed down from you. And I thank you (and Grandma) everyday for blessing me with the 'Green' genes. My wish is to be as active, as fit and as nimble as you are when I am in my late 70's. You inspire me every day with your ability to move and keep moving, and it is no wonder that I commit my heart and soul into all that I do when I see all you do and have always done for your local community, no matter where you have lived. They say the apple never falls far from the tree. Thank you for always being something to aspire to be and for understanding in the times when I am off following my dreams. Thank you for providing me with the source of life and for bringing me into this world so that I am able to do what I love doing.

To my stepfather, Frank Flanagan, you are the best stepfather I could ever ask for. Thank you for coming into my Mum's life when you did and for making her smile again. I am so grateful for all the times we have had together as a family and for all the support and love you have always given me.

To my father, Brian Jones for exposing me to the principles of 'Live Your Best Life' as a teenager, I trust you know the impact that it has had on my life? Dad, I am so grateful to you for always encouraging me to follow my dreams and providing me with the belief that it was possible. Love you Dad.

To my beautiful sister Leilani Jones, you inspire me in more ways than you have ever probably realised and I thank you always for your kind and beautiful heart. I love you for all that you bring into my life, into this world and am so grateful to call you my sister and always look forward to our times spent together.

Cathy Jones! Sister Sunshine, you truly have always been my ray of sunshine throughout all of my life; all I have is a full heart of love for you. You have always been there for me since the day I was born. When I count my blessings of gratitude, I always count you twice. You are my constant source of reminder that the small things are always the big things, because of all you do and have always done for me. From the laughter, the shitty times, the adventures and assisting me to bring my dreams to life, thank you for all that you do to keep the big wheels turning, personally and professionally. In my dreams I have always been 'Oprah' and you her trusty awesome assistant, and now we are bringing that dream to life.

To my best friend, Michelle McGinty, who has always believed in me, and who knew before anyone that I was always destined to do what I now do. Thank you for all the times in our high school years spent creating vision boards, writing in journals, sharing and updating our 5 year plans, keeping each other accountable, listening to my whacky beliefs and philosophies and all the many sleepless nights spent dreaming of our ideal average days. You always knew that one day I would meet Oprah! It is coming, I am sure! Lol. I love our moments in time spent together.

To Betty, Gordon & Jo Wilkinson (aka Mum, Dad & Sis), words can never express the gratitude in my heart for all that you do for David and I. I thank you for all that you do behind the scenes that makes things happen, for also loving me as your own daughter and sister, for believing in me, never questioning me (even when you think some of my ideas are truly out there) and for nurturing my dreams with as much love as I do. David and I are always grateful for all that you do. Thank you.

To my wonderful sexy man and husband, David, this book exists because you entered my life, and because you believed that what I had to say had to be shared with this world. Thank you for always believing in me and for being the soul who has partnered with me as we live our best lives together, we are 'Team Wilkinson' and I love all that we represent when together. Thank you for always challenging my thoughts and for not just looking into my eyes but looking through them into my heart and seeing my soul. You are love to me in every possible way.

Family cuddle times with our fur kids, Sushi and Sonny are my favourite.

# MY PASSION FOR COACHING:

# LET'S CREATE MAGIC TOGETHER

Whether it be you investing into you, or the organisation or company that you work for every day doing so, there is a definite and proven advantage for choosing to engage with and work with a coach.

More and more individual's these days are seeking out the Coach & Client partnership for all that it brings into their personal and professional lives.

The purpose of a coach has become somewhat of an evolutionary strategist.

Quite simply, a coach will ask you the questions you need to answer, which will assist you to define and to take action toward living your best life.

As we work together, we will de-clutter the noise, to filter through what is often information overload in your own head so that you can hear the essential things you need to in order to live well in today's world.

Through use of advanced communication and life skills we can get to the root of what truly matters, whilst connecting you to all planes within – the mental, physical and spiritual so that you feel a complete alignment across all areas of your life.

Learn ways in which you can feel great to absorb the constant change that surrounds you personally, in your workplace and within your career.

Let me ask you something…do you truly speak honestly with yourself and push yourself towards all you truly desire?

No. I didn't think so, and even if you do then I know you are always seeking more.

So, it is time to consider engaging your own personal or professional coach.

For You Corporation is my coaching company, a resource for personal and professional coaching. I am proud to say I am surrounded by a team of highly qualified and regarded coaches who subscribe to the techniques and 'Live Your Best Life™' philosophies presented in my book perform all coaching.

I work personally with an exclusive number of private clients each year, assisting them to breakthrough to success in their business and personal life so that they activate their own level of self-empowerment and fulfilment, and as a result become an inspiration to others.

If the messages in my book resonated with you and you would like to chat more with me about becoming a client, send me an email and we can schedule our first complimentary session together, where together we can decide how we move forward.

michele@foryoucorporation.com

# ABOUT THE "LIVE YOUR BEST LIFE™" 3 DAY PROFESSIONAL AND PERSONAL RETREAT PROGRAMS

Our flagship "Live Your Best Life™", 3 day professional and personal retreat programs are usually held in the most idyllic environment that's offered by beautiful Lake Macquarie, NSW, Australia. However, at the time of writing this book, we also host them in various locations across Australia.

Our "Live Your Best Life™" Retreat Programs give you an experience that will entirely change the course of your future with strategies to assist you to shape your best life.

Hosted by, Michele Jones and her team of purposely-selected coaches, this program is packed with loads of value, including the following, yet not limited to:

- Life coaching
- Business coaching
- Wellness coaching
- Coaching success strategies
- Professional Coach support
- Guest speakers
- Powerful communication techniques
- Critical thinking models
- Yoga and stretch classes
- Nutrition advice and cooking demonstrations
- An alignment of mind, body and spirit
- Thought provoking activities
- Personal development
- Team building solutions
- Guided visualisations
- 'Stuff' that is simply too good to mention here!

Along with many more tools, strategies and resources to guide you to creating your best life, whilst achieving long term sustainable results.

Much of the creative genius, processes and techniques that I share with you in this book are integrated and anchored deeply into the Retreat experience. Every single minute of the "Live Your Best Life" Retreat Program has been designed with this in mind, and everything that occurs on these Retreats serves a purpose to guide you closer to living and breathing your very best life.

These retreats are extremely powerful and continually provide people with all they need to create the change they truly desire in their life and/or business.

Over the 3 days you will be guided through a process that will assist you to explore, identify and reflect on what you really want in your life and/or business, and how to set about making real change. It isn't all an intellectual process, or one that you can attempt to logic to some extent, as one of the retreat philosophies is to offer all those who attend an experience; an experience that leads to deep-rooted transformation on all planes of mind, body and spirit and how this relates to all areas of your life.

Oh yeah and did I mention that they are also usually held on a houseboat?

A houseboat, I hear your say? Yes, that's right, a houseboat.

And why? Because I believe that there is so much to be learnt by being out in the elements of nature, all the lessons it provides and how this relates to your life.

For more information relating to the 'Live Your Best Life™' Retreat Programs and upcoming dates, please e-mail:

michele@foryoucorporation.com

# THE "LIVE YOUR BEST LIFE™" PHILOSOPHY

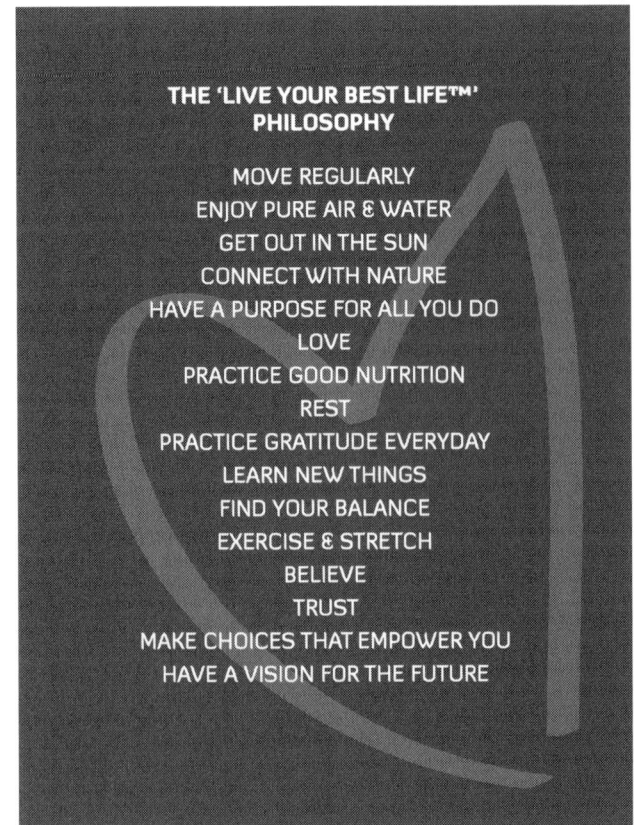

**THE 'LIVE YOUR BEST LIFE™' PHILOSOPHY**

MOVE REGULARLY
ENJOY PURE AIR & WATER
GET OUT IN THE SUN
CONNECT WITH NATURE
HAVE A PURPOSE FOR ALL YOU DO
LOVE
PRACTICE GOOD NUTRITION
REST
PRACTICE GRATITUDE EVERYDAY
LEARN NEW THINGS
FIND YOUR BALANCE
EXERCISE & STRETCH
BELIEVE
TRUST
MAKE CHOICES THAT EMPOWER YOU
HAVE A VISION FOR THE FUTURE

# GET YOUR VERY OWN COPY
# OF MY FIRST BOOK

'Bringing Life to Leadership' is based on almost thirty years of research, experience, application, observations and stories that explore the '5 Heartbeats of Great Leadership', bringing with it a fresh bold exploration on a topic that has held its strength and truth for 25 years or more. It pulls together an entire field for the reader, so no matter how many books you have read on leadership, this book will lead you to better understand these enduring time-tested and proven truths that hold constant regardless of context or circumstances.

No matter what your experience, age, generation or life stage, 'Bringing Life to Leadership' will remind you of the vital role that leaders play in our lives and our communities, it will also renew your interest in understanding what makes a great leader, rekindle your desire to be an inspiring yourself.

For nearly three decades Michele has assisted people to discover and develop their leadership potential whilst supporting one of the greatest leaders in the world she has ever met, her mentor, her friend, Shane Ward. This book will take you on a journey of their story, a story of incredible dedication, commitment and loyalty, and provide you with the social proof that growth, change and evolution are essential to achieving longevity in business and to enrich relationships, not only for themselves but also for those around them.

Find out what it means today – it will bring your heartbeat back into all you do by bringing the very essence of life to leadership, as this is a book leaders can use to do their real and necessary work, bringing about the essential charges that will renew organisation's and communities for years to come.

To order your personally signed copy, please contact Michele on: michele@foryoucorporation.com

Or for those of you, who simply can't wait and are living life in the electronic world, go directly to Amazon by copying and pasting this link:

http://www.amazon.com/Bringing-Life-Leadership-Proven-Heartbeats/dp/1502406683/ref=sr_1_2?ie=UTF8&qid=143 2770869&sr=8-2&keywords=Bringing+Life+to+Leadership

# BIG BUSINESS CLUBS

If you are interested in becoming a member of any of For You Corporation's 'Big Business Clubs', please be in touch and let me know how we can be of service to you.

Let me understand what your needs are, the results you are looking for in life and or business so I can match you to the group that will be of most value to you.

Contact me today at michele@foryoucorporation.com, so we can get you connected and started.

We have 4 unique clubs that we are extremely proud of.

# MEET THE AUTHOR

## Michele Jones

As an internationally renowned speaker and coach, I am the Master Coach and Owner of the For You Corporation, a full-service coaching company based in Australia, which is holistically devoted to assisting individuals, companies and businesses to create extraordinary lives and futures with fewer struggles.

As a dedicated professional, lifelong learner, educator, speaker, businesswoman, coach and now author of this, my second book 'Live Your Best Life', I bring a heartbeat to all that I do.

I am passionate about touching the lives of people around the world, and I am committed to guiding you to keep moving forward in life, towards achieving your very very best, because no matter who you are, I believe you all deserve to 'Live Your Best Life™'. And so much so that this has become my life's mantra, and I have committed my lifetime to it, it is my burning, passion and purpose and what I believe I was sent here to do.

I am sincere when I say that I believe your quality of life is a direct reflection of your thoughts and the choices that you make each day. I also believe that daily rituals do matter and that it is important to understand what negative emotions you are carrying around so that you can change the meaning of any event, give it new meaning and form new beliefs that will serve you better.

Gratitude is my elixir in life, there is always, always, always something to be grateful for...always, so, when I wake up in the morning I always express three things that I am thankful for and when I go to bed at night, I always acknowledge three things I have been grateful for that day. One thing I know for sure is that there is always someone somewhere that is much worse off than me; we really don't have much to be concerned about.

Over the years I believe I have been exposed to some of the greatest experiences in life, so it is no wonder my passion and zest for life is obvious.

I often wonder where did it all begin?

Was it growing up in the Australian outback and having to learn new life skills to survive from a young age?

Or from moving schools nearly every year of my life until I began my second year at high school?

Maybe it could have been my academic, sporting and acting pursuits throughout school and into my adult life?

Perhaps my years as a Youth Alderman and Mayor for my local council?

Did I obtain it when undertaking drama and theatre whilst being a Director for a young people's theatre group?

Could it even be contributed to my time serving in the Australian Army Reserves?

I have also attributed it to experiencing sexual abuse for twelve years as a child.

And then I think about the two-year period whereby I was awarded Young Australian of the Year?

It may have even been my eight-year journey to survive cervical cancer?

Or my life threatening stint with viral meningitis that left me having to learn to walk and talk again?

Or even, just maybe, my following challenges with obesity?

Some would say it might have had something to do with my stellar career of the past 25 years associated with one of the largest direct sales and marketing organisations in the globe.

And it could even be my educational pursuits in recent years to continue my own evolution to always provide more value no matter what I do.

I would even begin to say with great certainty that meeting and marrying the love of my life that makes everything have more meaning was a pivotal point in my life that every day leads to great things.

I do know that with such a variety of experiences, skill sets and situations that my greatest asset that has yielded me my biggest return on investment, be it personally or in business, is my mindset and outlook, along with my drive and passion to see organisation's, businesses and people to progress in life and move towards their own version of success and what living their best lives means to them.

So, where did it really all begin?

I now know to be true, after many years of searching for it, that it all began the day I was born…when I was gifted with this wonderful thing called innate wisdom, and the gift of life, no matter what it brings our way.

I have carried it around inside me for all the years of my soul's life so far, and just like you I am therefore always whole and complete and everything I need to journey with and experience in this lifetime is already within me, all I need to continually do is be open to it, listen to it and access it.

We all deserve to Live Our Best Life, every single one of us.

And I am ever so grateful to know, that is now something I do every single day.

My dream and my wish is that you will too.

# NOTES

# NOTES

# NOTES

# NOTES

# NOTES

# NOTES

# NOTES

# NOTES

Made in the USA
Charleston, SC
13 July 2015